THE
SKY ATLAS

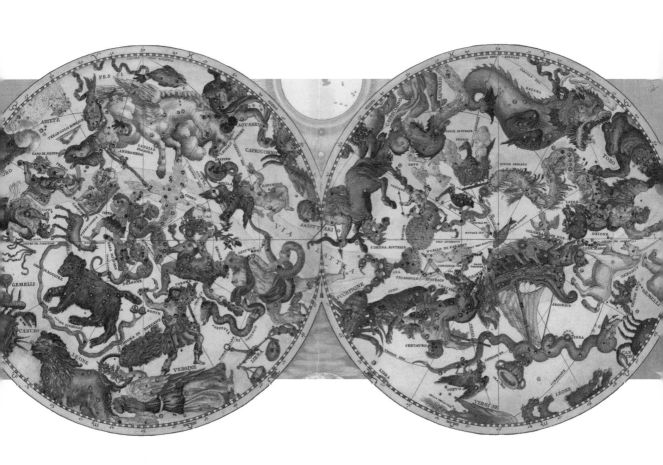

Allegory of the Planets and Continents
by Giovanni Battista Tiepolo, 1752.

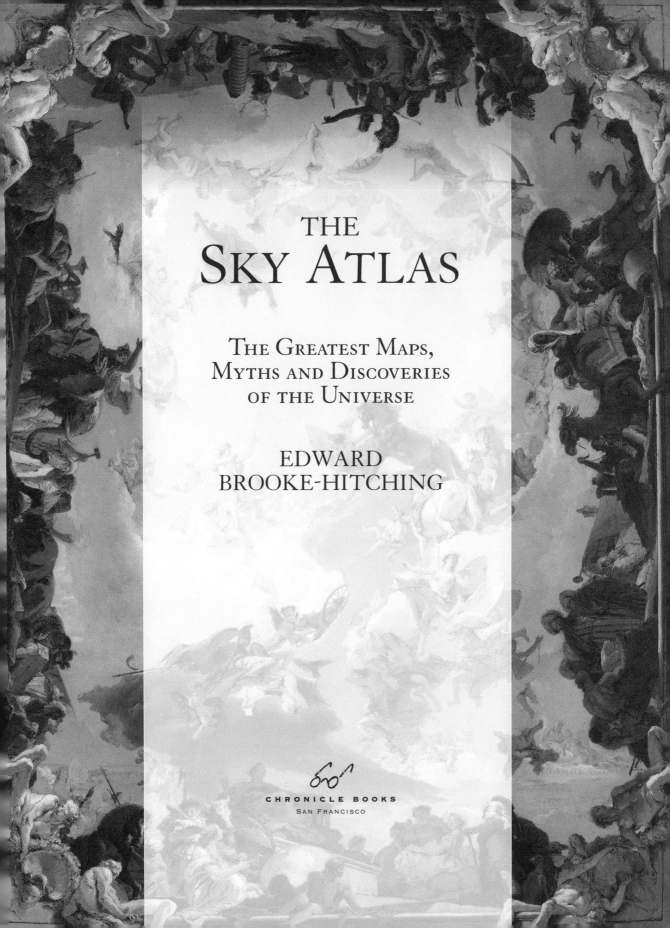

THE
SKY ATLAS

THE GREATEST MAPS, MYTHS AND DISCOVERIES OF THE UNIVERSE

EDWARD BROOKE-HITCHING

CHRONICLE BOOKS
SAN FRANCISCO

To Flavia Ebbisham
Sic itur ad astra

CONTENTS

ECLIPSE OF THE SUN.   THE ZODIACAL LIGHT.   THE MOON.   METEORIC SHOWER.

INTRODUCTION

The night sky, from Yaggy's Geographical Study *(1887).*

'When I follow the serried multitude of the stars in their circular course, my feet no longer touch the earth.'

PTOLEMY

What do we know of the beginnings of the universe? Really it depends on who you ask. A modern cosmologist will, of course, talk of the 'Big Bang', a theory that originated in 1927 with a Belgian priest named George Lemaître (see New Visions of the Universe: Einstein, Lemaître and Hubble entry on page 222), who posited the idea of there having been a 'cosmic egg' or 'primeval atom' from which the universe exploded into being. Billions of years ago all time, space and energy occupied a single infinitely dense, infinitely hot point known as the 'singularity'. In a trillion-trillionth of a second, this burst into expansion with a Big Bang and the universe came into existence, eventually ballooning to its current size of c.93 billion light years in diameter.

Ask another astrophysicist, and they could argue that this might not have been the *actual* beginning, as the theory is based on Einstein's general theory of relativity, which can only describe what happened after, not before, the singularity. In fact there are two Big Bang theories, and only one can be correct. The alternate suggests that the birth of space and time might have been even earlier, before the Bang, as part of a prior phase known as 'inflation', when the universe was dominated not by matter and radiation but by an energy inherent to itself – an as yet invisible 'dark energy' (see Breakthroughs of the Twentieth Century, and Beyond on page 232), hypothetical yet apparently observable through its effect. Turn to another astrophysicist for answers and they might point instead to the recent quantum equation models, working with Einstein's laws, that suggest there never was a creation point, that the universe may have existed forever with no beginning or end. (This position, incidentally, is the same one held by Aristotle (see The Ancient Greeks on page 50) more than 2300 years ago – for what could be greater evidence of the divine than the perfection of eternity?)

So… what exactly do we know of the beginnings of the universe? It is our oldest point of curiosity, the reason why we find creation myths at the root of cultures the world over. In Chinese mythology there is the first living being, P'an-ku, a furry horned giant who emerged from a cosmic egg after a wait of 18,000 years. P'an-ku cleaved the egg's shell in two with his axe to form the heavens and earth, and then fell apart himself. His limbs formed the mountains, his blood the rivers, his breath the wind.

Stephen Hawking was fond of illustrating his lectures with the belief of the Kuba people of the Democratic Republic of Congo, whose origin myth features the creator god Mbombo, or Bumba, a giant standing alone in darkness and water, who suffered a stomach pain and vomited up the Sun, Moon and stars. The Sun burnt away the waters, revealing the land. Mbombo then threw up nine kinds of animals and, with a final retch, man.

Elsewhere, in Hungarian mythology the Milky Way is called 'The Road of Warriors', a pathway down which Csaba,

A ceremonial dancing coat used by the shaman of the Koryak people, an indigenous culture of the Russian Far East. The coat is made of tanned reindeer skin and embroidered with disks of varying size representing constellations, with the belt sewn around the waist symbolizing the Milky Way.

the mythical son of Attila the Hun, will charge to the rescue should the Székelys (ethnic Hungarians living in Transylvania) be threatened. And nearly 4000 years ago in the region of modern Iraq, the ancient Babylonians had the *Enuma Elish* epic (see The Ancient Babylonians on page 26), which told of the universe resulting from a cosmic battle between monstrous primordial gods.

Consult the Bible (of which the Old Testament exhibits a clear influence from the *Enuma Elish*, with numerous

A fifteenth-century mandala (universal diagram) of the three-headed, four-armed Hevajra, enlightened being of Tibetan Buddhism, who appears here dancing with his consort Nairātmyā between four spiritual gateways at the centre of the cosmos.

narrative parallels) and the answers are provided in Genesis, with the Spirit of God moving on the face of the waters amid the darkness, before introducing light. Devoted faith in such biblical information has inspired interpretations with rigid literality in the past, leading to a number of curious results, whether it's the belief in a flat, square earth (see the Orlando Ferguson flat Earth map in The Ancient Greeks entry on page 53) or the long forgotten medieval belief in a sea above the sky, navigated by flying ships and sky sailors (see The Sea Above the Sky entry on page 98). In the seventeenth century, the archbishop James Ussher (1581–1656) went so far as to pinpoint the exact date and time of creation, deciding that it had occurred at about 6 p.m. on 22 October 4004 BC. In addition to this, the same century* also yielded an actual depiction of the pretemporal nothingness before the light of Creation, shown here by the physician and occultist Robert Fludd in his *Utriusque cosmi…* (1617).

In fact, it was reflecting on this Fludd image of the black void of pre-Creation – an image, one could argue, of the very

Robert Fludd's image of infinity from his Utriusque cosmi…, *1617.*

*For the most bizarre example of seventeenth-century Christian astronomical explanation there is the story of the Vatican librarian Leo Allatius, who allegedly wrote an unpublished treatise entitled *De praeputio Domini nostri Jesu Christi diatriba* ('A Discussion of the Foreskin of Our Lord Jesus Christ'), in which he claimed that the foreskin of the Son of God rose into the heavens and transformed into the rings of Saturn.

first 'sky' – that prompted the idea for this book. In essence, the aim was to collate a visual history of the sky, condensing the extensive and intricate worldwide histories of celestial mythology, philosophical cosmology, together with the landmark discoveries of astronomy and astrophysics, into a single illustrated journey through the millennia. While there is a variety of paintings, instruments and photographs gathered on these pages to illustrate the chronology of our gradual decoding of the cosmic theatre, primarily this is an atlas of celestial cartography.

To my mind, this is the most overlooked genre of mapmaking. In the history of cartography, reference works on the celestial map are vastly outnumbered by works focused on terrestrial cartography, despite the fact that the two genres were, traditionally, equally respected. Presumably this betrays an assumption that, while terrestrial maps portray the explorations and political machinations of monarchies and empires, maps of the world above reflect little of the world below. Indeed there can be a modern tendency to reduce star maps to the category of mere 'decorative' material, with a perceived paucity of historical substance. (Certainly, this is not helped by their historical association with the pseudoscience of astrology.) Paradoxically they also suffer from a perception as lifeless technical diagrams of interest only to the student scientist. As we shall see, in response to both charges, nothing could be farther from the truth. Celestial maps are as vibrant with story as any other – while often being peerless in their artistry.

Of course, the mapping traditions of celestial and terrestrial cartography are as different as the manner of discovery they represent. Terrestrial mapping is rooted in the gradual process of active exploration. From our initial forays into the unknown world, blank on the page, we recorded and measured our geographic expansion step-by-step and ship-by-ship across the terrestrial plain. The grand pageantry of the heavens, on the other hand, was always on full glorious display from the very beginning. Against the countless visible stars, the Sun, Moon and wandering planets carried out their actions and phases openly, yet in total mystery.

To celestial cartographers, faced with such overwhelming vastness, the sky was itself a canvas for the projection of every myth, fear and religious fantasy in the mind of its observer, as the human brain searched restlessly for recognizable patterns in the chaos. With no vessels of exploration to probe this greatest of oceans, the astronomer–artists could only draw on what they knew – their gods, myths and animals – and apply them to the constellations prominent in their order of brightness. Hence the twelve signs of the zodiac are older than written record, used by the ancient Romans, who inherited the concept from the Greeks. They, in turn, drew the idea from the Babylonians, and so on, back into the murk of prehistory.

Though this book opens with a gathering of prehistoric relics from the field of archaeoastronomy, it is with the ancient Sumerians and Babylonians of Mesopotamia that the story of recorded astronomy begins (as we discover, for example, that the first named author in history was a lunar priestess). The journey then takes us across to ancient Egypt, and on to unravel the various spectacular celestial concepts of the ancient Greek philosophers. The most wonderful and enduring of these early Hellenistic ideas is the concept of the crystalline spheres (see Capturing the Cosmos: Clockwork

A zodiac wheel from Astrolabium Planum *by Johannes Angelus, after 1491.*

and the Printing Press entry on page 104), the idea that the
world exists within a nested hierarchy of increasingly large
and transparent, but physical, spheres, each one supporting a
planet, the Sun or Moon, against a backdrop of the 'fixed stars'.
As bizarre as it seems to us, the idea does have an obvious logic,
as it accounts for the travelling motions of the celestial bodies
by extrapolating the known behaviour of the terrestrial realm
– for something to move endlessly on such a long journey, it
must surely be because it is carried.

In fact the story of the heavenly spheres illustrates a
notable point that one comes to realize applies to much of
the history of astronomy. The true breakthroughs were often
made precisely by *disregarding* the obvious, the learned and
logical; and reaching instead for a theory counterintuitive
in its originality. Perhaps the most famous champion of this
approach is Copernicus (see Islamic Celestial Works entry
on page 78), by his tearing of Earth from the centre of God's
created universe to replace it with the Sun, sending seismic
shocks through contemporary religious and social institutions
and triggering the scientific revolution. Arguably the most
important instrument of astronomers, we discover, is the
imagination, as they pursue the ultimate goal of attaining an
objective viewpoint of the universe, to best survey the intricacy
of its mechanics.

This is why the stories of erroneous astronomical ventures,
or scientific myth, are collected here alongside the great
discoveries and the assorted cultural myths in this book –
whether it's Percival Lowell's observations of alien-made
canals on Mars (see Percival Lowell Spies Life on Mars entry
on page 210), René Descartes's notion of a 'full' space of
swirling vortices (see The Cartesian Universe entry on page 142),
or curious escapades like the hunt for the phantom planet
Vulcan (see The Phantom Planet: Vulcan entry on page 198).
We learn as much from these ultimately disproven flights of
imagination and interpretation as we do from the triumphs.
And in step with this march of progress (and its occasional
diversion) we see the celestial cartographic art, as the pictorial
record of these innovations, flourish with the invention of the
Gutenberg printing press and, along with the cartographic
art as a whole, explode in popularity with the Renaissance
passion for measurement and accurate depiction of form. The
Age of Discovery, which opened in the fifteenth century, was

also the golden age of cartography. Just as the discoveries of new nations and continents filled maps with increasing detail and sense of scale, so too did discoveries of the sky, together with diagrams of the battling theories as to the structure of the cosmos. The celestial atlas reached a particular artistic highpoint in the seventeenth century, with the publication of Andreas Cellarius's *Atlas coelestis* (see Newtonian Physics entry on page 156), commonly agreed to be the most beautiful sky atlas ever created.

In astronomy, the mysteries were unravelled further with the later development of spectroscopy, as it was realized that the stars telegraph their chemical secrets via the spectrum of the light they emit. Out of this the science of astrophysics emerged, and the scope of celestial mapping transformed with the coinciding development of photography. With the innovations of the twentieth century, the rate of discovery hit a new velocity with, for example, the search for universally applicable laws, most famously featuring Albert Einstein's theory of general relativity (see New Visions of the Universe entry on page 224), that would influence the aforementioned 'cosmic egg' idea of Monsignor Lemaître. With Edwin Hubble (see New Visions of the Universe entry on page 231) subsequently finding that the glowing nebulae in the sky are,

The Aboriginal constellation Emu in the Sky is made not of stars but of the darkness between them. Here it is viewed from Mount Arapiles, Victoria, Australia.

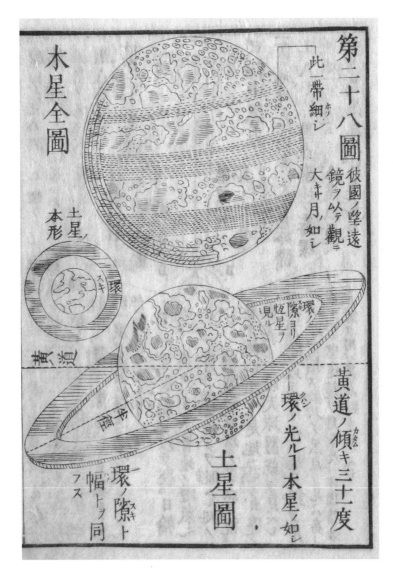

From Kopperu Tenmon Zukai, *1808, by the Japanese artist Shiba Kōkan, who introduced the heliocentric theory of Nicolaus Copernicus to Japan.*

in fact, entire galaxies of stars lying far beyond the boundaries of the Milky Way and that, in addition, many of these galaxies were racing away from us, the model of the expanding universe was proven. Only in 1998 was it found that, contrary to previous thinking, this expansion is not slowing down but speeding up, that the galaxies are racing away from each other, which is as puzzling a discovery as tossing a stone into the air and watching it fly at increasing speed away from you. Exactly why this is happening is a mystery, but by calculating the rate of expansion and working backwards we were able to put a figure to the age of the universe at somewhere between 10 and 20 billion years. Just over 350 years since Archbishop

Ussher's estimate of a 5650 year-old universe, with the help of the Hubble Space Telescope we have refined the modern figure to 13.8 billion years and, astonishingly, are now able to lay our eyes on galaxies of almost that light-travel distance, like GN-z11 (see Breakthroughs of the Twentieth Century, and Beyond entry on page 234) in the Ursa Major constellation, which existed just 400 million years after the Big Bang.

And so we arrive back at our first – or rather, *the* first – question: what exactly do we know of the origins of the universe? Well we know that with each day we venture deeper into the open heart of the mystery, as space probes cross the frontier of interstellar space and push back the shadows like the oceanic explorers of old.* We know that, with orbital space telescopes extending our gaze with unprecedented acuity, the days of solving the myriad riddles tied to this primary question – the possibility of life outside our world, the fabric and fate of our universe – grow closer too, if we can survive to see them. From history, we've learnt that we should maintain a healthy scepticism of everything we think we know, for even our assumption of there being only one universe could be as myopic as that of the astronomer of 100 years ago, who *knew* the solar system to be the only galaxy.

There are two things, though, that I think are certain. The first is that it is our scientific and philosophical imagination that will remain our most useful tool, as it was for those who devised the lenses for the first telescope, rearranged the planets on the page or encapsulated the grandeur of the universe with a chalkboard of equations. The other certainty is the immortal life of the celestial map. The images in this book show just how differently we have mapped the sky across time and cultures, while through their mere existence demonstrating just how similar has been our determination to do so. In whatever advanced astrophotographic form cartography will take in the future, however far we move away from the prehistoric ancestor daubing the first star charts on the walls of caves, it will always be with maps that we draw the record of our accomplishments, and mark the way for the rest to follow.

---

*For example it was only in July 2018 that researchers at the University of Cambridge discovered, using data from the European Space Agency's Gaia satellite, that 8–10 billion years ago a dwarf galaxy named the 'Gaia Sausage' collided with the Milky Way. The Sausage was entirely obliterated, while the Milky Way was reshaped through the addition of stars, gas and dark matter, resulting in its distinctive bulge.

THE ANCI

The ancient Chinese feudal state of Qi was very small in size. It's rarely mentioned in official records, and when it is it's usually with the note that 'its affairs are not worth mentioning'. However, the state is remembered to this day as the origin of a popular Chinese idiom used to dismiss baseless concerns, *Qǐ rén yōu tiān* ('the people of Qi worry about the sky'), which refers to how the Qi people went about their daily lives perpetually anxious that the heavens could fall down and crush them at any moment.

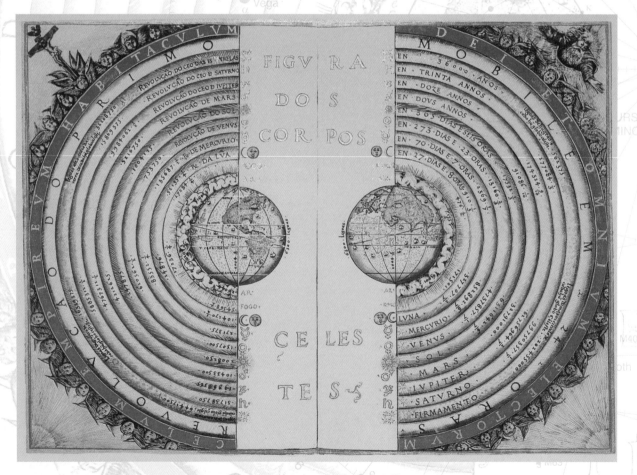

'Astronomy compels the soul to look upward, and leads us from this world to another.' Plato, *Republic* (c.380 BC)

Like this relic of ancient belief glinting in present-day language, the history of our response to the sky striates the mass of modern culture, for the heavens have always been a source of wonder. In its arena we have found gods, monsters, the measurement of time, chemical secrets and divine warnings; all imbued with the dread weight of overhead cosmic endlessness. It's a mesmerism that holds true today, for the more of its secrets we decode the more layers of new mystery we discover and the deeper we are drawn in. The documented history of how we interrogated the heavens begins with the Sumerians as we shall find a bit later, but what of the time before record? What was the nature of our connection with the prehistoric sky?

Archaeoastronomy is the name for this field of study, which should be clearly differentiated from the later scholarly traditions of ancient astronomy. This is the attempt to decipher the enigmatic relationships that prehistoric people had with the sky, through the scant surviving material evidence. Recently, particularly in Europe, discoveries of ancient astronomical artefacts have helped to enhance our picture of the Neolithic and Bronze Age inhabitants as a people in possession of a more sophisticated knowledge of mathematics and astronomy than previously thought, long before the invention of writing systems or optical instruments to aid observation.

The elk skin sky map of the Native American Pawnee people. Stars are drawn in different sizes to represent their order of magnitude (brightness).

OPPOSITE: *Figure of the Heavenly Bodies, (c.1568) by the Portuguese cosmographer and mapmaker Bartolomeu Velho, illustrating the Ptolemaic universe.*

PREHISTORIC STARGAZING

In 1940, near the village of Montignac in southwestern France, a pet dog named Robot led a group of teenagers to discover one of the greatest collections of prehistoric artwork ever found, via a small hole that led to the Lascaux caves. Inside they found a 'cavalcade of animals larger than life painted on the walls and ceiling of the cave', recalled Marcel Ravidat, one of the teens, who added that 'each animal seemed to be moving'. More than 600 wall paintings, using mineral pigments, and nearly 1500 engravings covered the interior walls and ceilings of the caves nicknamed 'the prehistoric Sistine Chapel'. The combined efforts of many generations, the artwork was estimated to have been created some 17,000 years ago. There were several areas to the caves: the Hall of the Bulls, which featured a bull

A section of the Hall of the Bulls from the Lascaux caves, France. The black markings are believed to be a prehistoric mapping of the Pleiades star cluster.

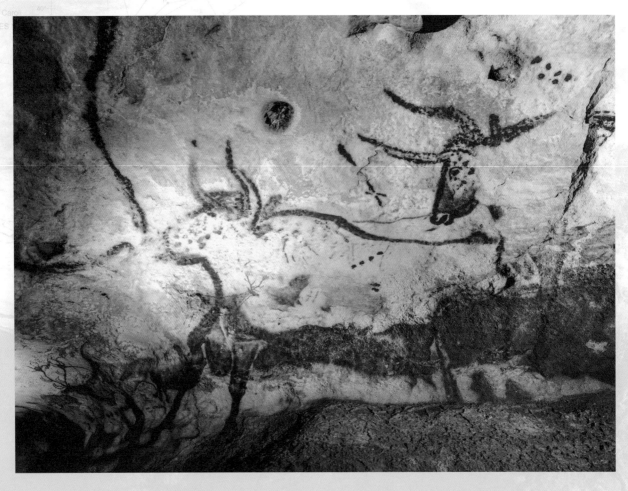

painting 17ft (5.2m) long, the largest animal discovered so far in cave art; the Lateral Passage; the Shaft of the Dead Man; the Chamber of Engravings; the Painted Gallery; and the Chamber of Felines. The animal drawings appeared to have a calendrical nature, as the majority had seasonal characteristics: the deer were shown in their autumnal rutting season, the horses at times of mating and foaling. (Curiously, though, there was not a single depiction of a reindeer, which was the principal food source for the artists at that time.)

Of particular interest was the drawing of a bull, a bird and a bird-man on the wall of the Shaft of the Dead Man. This has been interpreted by Dr Michael Rappenglueck of the University of Munich, and others, to be the earliest existing star map, the three figures representing the stars Vega, Deneb and Altair in a grouping known today as the Summer Triangle. These three are among the brightest objects discernible in the night sky during the middle months of the northern summer. Elsewhere in the cave, in the Hall of the Bulls, another diagram appeared to depict the Pleiades star cluster, sometimes called the Seven Sisters. Small dabs of paint in other parts of the picture might also have represented smaller stars. The cave was opened to the public in 1948, but this exposure to touch and breath altered the internal environment, and the cave was closed in 1963 as a protective measure. Today, one can visit Lascaux II, a replica built just down the road from the original. As a kind of prehistoric planetarium, the Lascaux artwork allows us to view the cosmos through Ice Age eyes.

Interpreting the sky for measurement of time also appears to be a technique that predates the invention of writing. Take for example the Mesolithic 'calendar' monument at Warren Field, Scotland, created c.8000 BC, a site examined today by those searching for the beginning of the concept of time. Spotted from the air and excavated in 2004, the twelve pits seem to mimic the phases of the Moon to follow the lunar months, and align along the southeast horizon for the sunrise of the midwinter solstice. The latter feature would have provided the hunter-gatherers with an annual 'astronomic correction' to better track the passing of time and the seasonal changes, symbolically and practically. This is the earliest example of such a celestial timekeeping structure – no known comparable site would exist throughout Europe for several thousands of years.

The first image of Stonehenge drawn on site, c.1573, by the Flemish painter Lucas de Heere.

The British Isles is especially rich in Mesolithic monuments: in the development of the Stonehenge monument,* erected sometime between 3000 BC and 2000 BC, there was also an axis generally oriented towards the summer solstice sunrise, and the winter solstice in the other. 'For my own part', wrote the Victorian astronomer Norman Lockyer (1836–1920), 'I consider that the view that our ancient monuments were built to observe and to mark the rising and setting places of the heavenly bodies is now fully established.' The astronomical function of Stonehenge was self-evident to Lockyer; however, despite its popularity, the theory that Stonehenge was an ancient observatory remains only a theory. Recent research into the inner circle of bluestones has suggested an alternative function – that the inner circle of bluestones were chosen for their acoustic properties when struck with rocks, which would explain why local stones were disregarded, in favour of hauling the bluestones into place from Pembrokeshire, more than

OPPOSITE: *The earliest surviving picture of Stonehenge, one of a number of drawings accompanying an abridged manuscript version of Wace's* Roman de Brut, *made in Britain 1338–1340.*

*Stonehenge, incidentally, is not technically a henge. This is defined as earthworks consisting of a circular banked enclosure with an internal ditch – Stonehenge's bank is inside its ditch.

180 miles (290km) away. Near to this source point, the village church of Maenclochog is said to have used bluestone bells into the eighteenth century.

Another likelihood, if separate and not directly linked, was that Stonehenge served as a burial mound, as large deposits of human bone have been buried there from the time of its establishment over a period of 500 years. And, in fact, this connection with ritual burial and sky worship is spread across cultures from ancient history to modern day – the Zoroastrians of pre-Islamic Persia would build 'Towers of Silence', tall circular structures on which the bodies of the deceased would be placed to be picked apart by carrion birds. In Tibet, meanwhile, a similar tradition continues to be practised. The Tibetan 'sky burial', in which the corpse is placed on a mountaintop also for the birds to devour, is part of the Vajrayana Buddhism belief that, once the soul has left, the body is merely an empty vessel to be disposed of. Offering it up to the sky and its wildlife is considered the most generous way of doing so.

Turning from sky sites to cosmological objects, another remarkable find was made in 1999, when two grave robbers armed with a metal detector uncovered a Bronze Age treasure trove at a site near Nebra, Saxony-Anhalt, in Germany. Among the small pile of two bronze swords, two hatchets, a chisel and pieces of spiral bracelets they found a unique object, a bronze disc 12in (30cm) in diameter, oxidized to a glowing blue-green patina and inlaid with symbols of gold. The looters (who were later prosecuted and, on appealing for leniency, had their sentences increased) sold the stash to an underground antiquities dealer in Cologne, and for two years the disc and its burial companions changed hands on the black market. It wasn't until 2002, when the disc was recovered by authorities after a sting operation led by Dr Harald Meller of the Museum of Halle in Germany, that the true significance of the Nebra sky disc began to be realized.

Through radiocarbon analysis of the axes and swords with which it was buried, the disc has been associatively dated to c.1600 BC and the Bronze Age Unetice culture. This means that the Nebra sky disc is verified as the oldest confirmed depiction of the cosmos in existence – an astounding

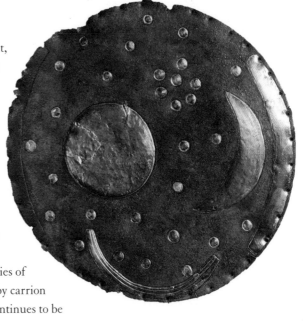

ABOVE: *The Nebra sky disc, unearthed in 1999 in the German state of Saxony-Anhalt, and associatively dated to c.1600 BC.*

discovery that questions the traditional thinking of Bronze
Age Europe as a place of intellectual darkness in the shadow
of the enlightened cultures of ancient Egypt and Greece. The
disc has a surprising sophistication: its inlaid symbols clearly
include the Sun and Moon, and, while these are surrounded
by an apparently random sprinkle of stars, the prominent
stellar grouping just north of the centre was recognized as the
Pleiades cluster, just as they would have shone in the Bronze
Age sky over northern Europe.

Even more intriguing are the interpretations of the two curved
golden bands (one of which is missing) along its edges. These
span 82 degrees, which matches the angle the Sun is seen to
travel along the horizon between the high midsummer sunset
and the low midwinter sunset. In other words, the disc might
well have been a functional device to mark the solstices precisely
as they would have occurred in Nebra, which would have been
of significant use for agriculture. The third golden arc, distinctive
in that it curves upwards away from the edges, has been variously

*A composite image of the Pleiades
star cluster, captured between
1986 and 1996 at the Palomar
Observatory, California.*

interpreted as the Milky Way, or perhaps a rainbow. The leading theory, however, has thrilling implications. Might the golden curve represent a 'solar barge' or 'sun boat', the vessel that transported the sun-god Ra during the night according to Egyptian mythological tradition? Could the sphere of ancient Egyptian cultural influence have spread this far at this time?

The idea of such international involvement is not as far-fetched as it seems. A geochemical survey conducted in 2011 found that, while the copper elements of the disc could be traced to local mines, the gold and tin content of the bronze were identified as originating from Cornwall, England, a distance of more than 700 miles (1127km) as the crow flies. The disc reveals not just an overlooked sophistication of its authorial culture, but also the existence of a substantial metal trade from the British Isles towards central Germany, and perhaps even Egyptian mythological inspiration, if it is indeed a solar vessel depicted. Little wonder, then, that in 2013 the Nebra sky disc was designated by the United Nations Educational, Scientific and Cultural Organization (UNESCO) as 'one of the most important archaeological finds of the twentieth century'.

ABOVE: *The 150ft (46m) Nazca Line spider, one of the famous set of geoglyphs cut into the Nazca Desert in southern Peru sometime between 500 BC and 500 AD. No record of their purpose exists, but it is believed they're linked to the presence of water, suggesting the images are likely messages of thanks to the sun-gods.*

LEFT: *The unique 'Berlin Gold Hat', a ceremonial hat of embossed gold dating to the Late Bronze Age, c.1000–800 BC, found in southern Germany or Switzerland. A Bronze Age interpreter could use it as a solar and lunar calendar, predicting lunar eclipses and other celestial events.*

THE ANCIENT BABYLONIANS

As fascinating as it is to examine these prehistoric discoveries, ultimately any definitive conclusion as to their astronomical nature is hampered by the lack of supporting documentation. The interpretations of their celestial significance are modern, driven by our zeal to trace evidential foundations of early celestial knowledge. For the earliest records-based research, we need to move from Europe farther east.

Western astronomy originated with the Sumerians, the supremely inventive people in southern Mesopotamia (modern southern Iraq) who devised, among other innovations, the

Nicolaes Visscher's map of ancient Babylon, 1660.

modern practice of dividing a circle into 360 degrees, each of sixty minutes, and the earliest known system of writing – cuneiform – dating to c.3500–3200 BC. The task of studying and examining the sky on behalf of the monarchs fell to the 'EN', the position of high priest or priestess that carried with it great political power. The most famous character to hold this title (c.2354 BC) was Enheduanna, daughter of King Sargon of Akkad, who was the first woman appointed to the role. Today she is remembered for the poetry and hymns she composed relating details of her life, particularly the 153-line work *Nin-me-šara* ('The Exaltation of Inanna') which features her lunar observations as priestess to the Moon goddess Nanna. As such, Enheduanna is considered the first named author in history.

As Sumer fell from power c.2000 BC, the Babylonian civilization grew under the conqueror-king Hammurabi. The Sumerian language was gradually replaced with Akkadian, but many of the Sumerians' advanced traditions fed into the younger Babylonian culture – most notably astronomy. As with other ancient cultures, early Babylonian astronomy was an attempt to impose order on chaos, a rigorous scientific analysis of the heavens powered by the unscientific motive that, in part, drove astronomy for the next 3000 years – divination. The Babylonians associated their gods with the stars and planets, and great value was placed on the interpretation of the behaviour of the heavenly bodies. Those who were able to read the stars could hold real influence over terrestrial affairs.

This universal theme of searching for patterns in the chaos of the cosmos extended to the Babylonian creation myth *Enuma Elish*, possibly composed as early as the eighteenth century BC. Fragments of the story were discovered in 1849 amid the ruins of the Library of Ashurbanipal at Nineveh (Mosul, Iraq) by the English archaeologist Austen Henry Layard. In about a thousand lines of Sumero-Akkadian, written across seven tablets, the epic relates the birth of the universe, 'When the sky above was not named', as the waters of two primeval gods Abzu (representing fresh water) and Tiamat (oceans) mingled to bring about the great Creation. Several new gods came into being inside Tiamat's belly, one of whom produced a son, Marduk, who was given power over the wind and caused havoc by creating tornadoes. Abzu grew irritated with these gods and planned to kill them, but they

The Tower of Babel *by Marten van Valckenborch, 1595. The myth, told in Genesis, was used to explain the global variety of languages. Following the Great Flood, humanity migrated eastwards to the land of Shinar, where they spoke a single language and arrogantly started building a tower tall enough to reach Heaven. In response God confused their speech and scattered them around the world. The tower has been associated by historians with structures known to have existed, most notably the Etemenanki, a ziggurat (rectangular stepped tower) 300ft (91m) high, dedicated to the Mesopotamian god Marduk by Nabopolassar, the king of Babylonia c.610 BC. Alexander the Great ordered it to be demolished c.331 BC.*

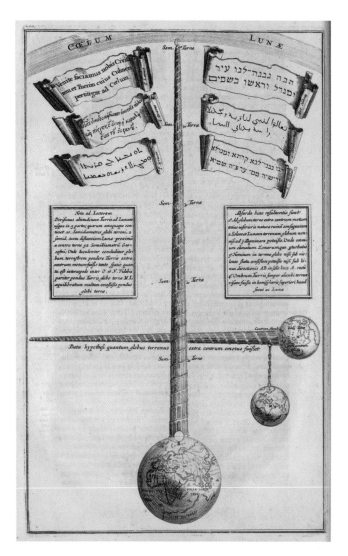

OPPOSITE: *A bas-relief scene from the ancient Assyrian city of Nimrud, which has been interpreted as showing the god Marduk's victory over the cosmic leviathan Tiamat.*

LEFT: *Athanasius Kircher published* Turris Babel *in 1679, demonstrating the impossibility of the Tower of Babel touching Heaven by analyzing the height required.*

pre-emptively launched a successfully lethal attack. Tiamat was moved to avenge Abzu's death, but Marduk was anointed as the leader of the gods within her, and with newfound power he defeated Tiamat, tearing her body in half. Thus were created the earth and skies. In a final formalizing act, Marduk also created the calendar, and arranged the Sun, Moon and stars in an orderly manner. The myth elevated the Babylonian god Marduk to superiority over other Mesopotamian deities, and serves to provide us with an idea of the scenes that played out in the mind of the ancient Babylonians as they gazed upwards – especially when catching a glimpse of the flickering Jupiter, with which Marduk, the 'bull calf of the sun-god', was astrologically associated.

The earliest astronomical texts in existence are Babylonian, the oldest being the Venus tablet of Ammisaduqa, which dates to the reign of King Ammisaduqa in the mid-seventeenth century BC. The cuneiform tablet is a record of twenty-one years of careful observations of the heliacal risings and settings (when a star or planet is visible on the eastern horizon just before and after sunrise) of Venus.*

The tablet is just one of a set of seventy in the collection of astronomical diaries known collectively as the *Enuma Anu Enlil*, which largely detail observed celestial omens, and the subsequent divinatory interpretations offered by contemporary priest–scribes, usually referred to as Chaldaeans. These records were maintained well into the first millennium BC, and provide a wealth of astronomical and historical material, documenting, for example, the most seismic event

ABOVE: *A reconstructed calcite disc found by the British archaeologist Sir Leonard Woolley during excavations of the Sumerian city of Ur. It depicts a sacrificial scene, with high-priestess Enheduanna third from the right.*

*A curious fact about Venus is that it rotates so slowly, at 4.05mph (6.52km/h), that you could stroll across its surface at the same speed as the Sun passes through its sky. This means – in the words of astrobiologist David Grinspoon – 'you could watch the sunset forever just by walking.' This is assuming, of course, that you managed to avoid being crushed by its dense, heavy atmosphere, and that you weren't instantly boiled up by the planet's average temperature of 460°C (860°F).

of that period in the region – the conquest of Alexander the Great. One tablet, discovered in 1880, records the battle of Gaugamela on 1 October 331, when Alexander defeated the Achaemenid king Darius III and conquered Mesopotamia. As recounted in the cuneiform, the Chaldaeans had anticipated such an outcome, having read the sky eleven days earlier and recorded: 'There was a lunar eclipse. Its totality was covered at the moment when Jupiter set and Saturn rose. During totality the west wind blew, during clearing the east wind. During the eclipse, deaths and plague occurred.'

After detailing Darius's loss to the 'king of the world' (Alexander) following this ominous celestial event, the Chaldaean writes: 'The significance is: The son of the king will become purified for the throne but will not take the throne. An intruder will come with the princes of the west; for eight years he will exercise kingship; he will conquer the enemy army; there will be abundance and riches on his path;

BELOW: *The Fall of Babylon, John Martin's 1831 painting of Cyrus the Great defeating the Chaldaean army.*

he will continually pursue his enemies; and his luck will not run out.' The first-century AD Roman historian Quintus Curtius Rufus notes in his *Histories of Alexander the Great* that Darius desperately performed additional sacrifices before the battle but, with such a decisive statement by the heavens, no preparatory ritual could save him – not even the last-resort method to trick the gods that was reportedly favoured by King Esarhaddon, who reigned over the Neo-Assyrian Empire 681–669 BC. So terrified was Esarhaddon of lunar eclipses that he would install a substitute king (chosen from prisoners or the mentally ill) on the throne for a few days to bear the brunt of the gods' anger until the event passed. Esarhaddon then executed the man, to be certain that any residual ill portent was cleared away.

Opposite: The Venus tablet of Ammisaduqa, the earliest existing record of Mesopotamian astronomical observations, dated to around the mid-seventeenth century BC. It recorded the first and last times the planet Venus was visible on the horizon in relation to sunrise and sunset.

Left: The zodiac and its recognizable symbols trace back to the ancient Sumerians, later to be adopted by the Babylonians, Egyptians and Greeks. This limestone kudurru (boundary stone) from c.1125–1100 BC invokes nine gods, including the sun-god Shamash (represented with the solar disc) and the seventeen divine symbols thought to be zodiacal constellations, which the Sumerians called The Shining Herd.

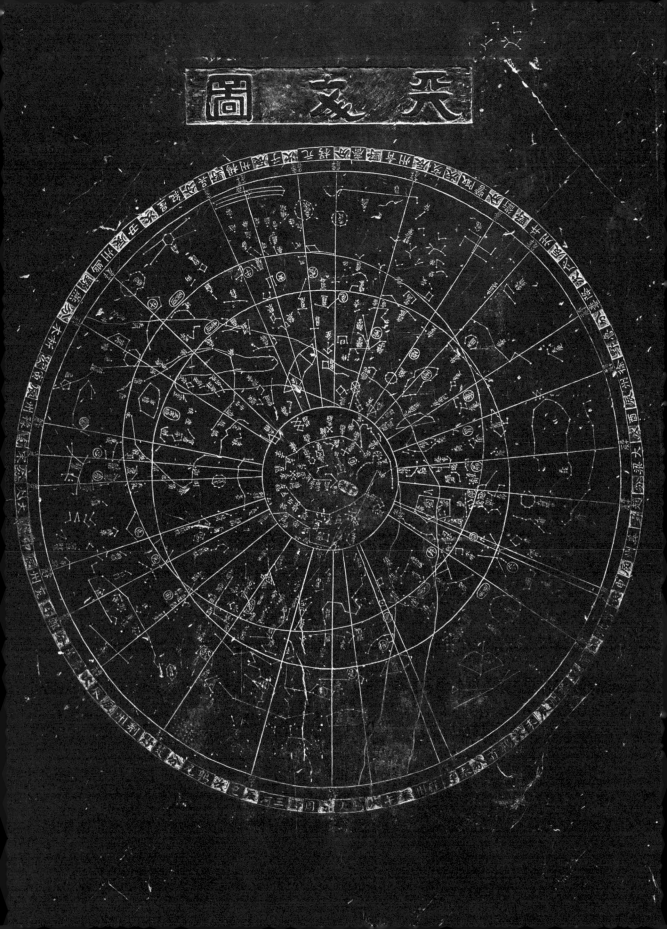

A rare rubbing of the Suzhou astronomical chart by Huang Shang, an extraordinary work of early Chinese science, created in 1193 and lost centuries ago. Fortunately it was etched into stone in 1247 by Wang Zhiyuan for preservation. The star map shows 1434 stars grouped into 280 asterisms, with the accompanying text listing a total of 1565 known stars. 'Before the Great Absolute had unfolded itself', begins the text, 'the three primal essences, Heaven, Earth and Man, were involved within it. This was termed original chaos because the intermingled essences had not yet separated. When the Great Absolute unfolded, the light and pure formed Heaven, the heavy and impure formed Earth, and the mingled pure and impure formed Man. The light and pure constitute spirit, the heavy and impure constitute body, and the union of body and spirit constitute Man.'

THE SKY-WATCHERS OF ANCIENT CHINA

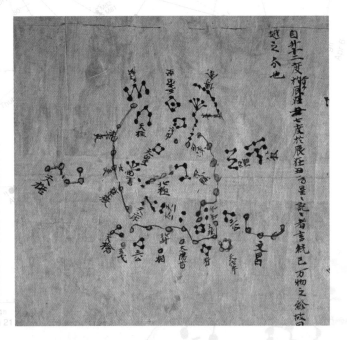

A detail of the North Polar region from the Dunhuang star map. This chart is thought to date from the reign of Emperor Zhongzong of Tang (AD 705–710); in its entirety, the document contains 1300 stars.

Far before the development of astronomy in Europe, or indeed any culture around the world, in ancient China there were the concepts of *lifa* ('calendrical methods') and *tianwen* ('celestial patterns'). Both practices involved the study and interpretation of the stars and celestial phenomena, but for two different ends. Those who engaged in *lifa* read the skies to find regular and predictable patterns, to distil order from the overwhelming quantity of the heavens and establish a structured calendar for the inhabited world (known as *tianxia*, 'That which is below heaven'). *Tianwen*, on the other hand, had more in common with the ancient Roman *prodigia* (unusual occurrences in the natural world thought to be omens of divine wrath – see The Sea Above the Sky entry on page 101). Practitioners of *tianwen* would scour the skies for the extraordinary, recording bizarre phenomena, creating dictionaries of sky language and interpreting the significance of these supernatural messages.

Around the world in the nineteenth century, China was referred to as the Celestial Empire, and indeed the history of China's national identity is entwined with the heavens. The job of studying *lifa* and *tianwen* was performed by members of the

ABOVE: *The creation of the River of Heaven (the Milky Way), part of a Chinese legend of the romance between a Weaver Girl (the star Vega) and a lowly Cowherd (the star Altair).*

LEFT: *The Yutu ('Jade Rabbit') faces off against Sun Wukong, the immortal Monkey King. The rabbit of Chinese folklore that lives on the Moon is also commonly depicted with a pestle and mortar, churning an elixir for the goddess of the Moon, Chang'e (in Japanese and Korean mythology, the rabbit grinds rice cakes instead.) The modern Chinese space programme honoured this cultural history by naming the Chinese Lunar Exploration Programme 'Chang'e', and the lunar rover it sent to the Moon in 2013 Yutu.*

imperial civil service, as control over such interpretations was vital to the state. From the time of the Zhou dynasty (1046–256 BC), Chinese emperors ruled with the seal of celestial approval known as the Mandate of Heaven, and were bestowed with the title of *Tian Zi* ('Son of Heaven'). Though this benefited new sovereigns with divine authority, it also came with risk. Without proper guidance, instances of frightening *tianwen* – be they comets, storms, floods, etc. – could be read by the people as signs of celestial disapproval of their rulers, and rebellion might ensue. The interpreters of *tianwen*, too, faced great risk, especially in the prediction of solar eclipses, which were believed to be the Sun devoured by a giant sky dragon* – indeed, the earliest Chinese word for eclipse, shih, meant 'to eat'. It was a sign of great doom for the ruling emperor. (By c.20 BC, records tell us that Chinese astrologers understood the cause of eclipses, and by 8 BC predictions were made of total solar eclipse based on the 135-month recurrence period. By AD 206, Chinese astrologers could forecast solar eclipses by reading the motion of the Moon.) A surviving quotation in reference to the eclipse of 2136 BC reveals the fate of two astronomers who failed to anticipate the event:

> Here lie the bodies of Ho and Hi,
> Whose fate, though sad, is risible;
> Being slain because they could not spy
> Th' eclipse which was invisible.

For thousands of years the Chinese studied the skies in an uninterrupted scientific odyssey. The astronomer Shi Shen of the fourth century BC is one of the earliest named, credited with positioning the 121 stars that one finds marked in surviving early texts. It was Shi who recorded making the earliest deliberate sunspot observations, which he believed to be eclipses. This is sometimes attributed to a contemporary, Gan De, c.364 BC, of the aforementioned state of Qi, but Gan had his own discoveries to his name. He made the first detailed observations of Jupiter, for example, and described a 'small reddish star' beside the planet, which the astronomical historian Xi Zezong claimed was the first naked-eye observation of the

Chinese oracle bone carved between 1600 BC and 1050 BC.

Reverse side of the oracle bone.

---

*The idea of a devouring creature is a common mythical explanation for the eclipse among cultures. The Vikings saw sky wolves chasing the Moon – an eclipse occurring when one of the animals successfully caught it. (The English word 'eclipse' comes from the Greek *ekleipō* meaning disappearance, or abandonment.) The phenomenon carried the terrible message that the gods had forsaken mankind.

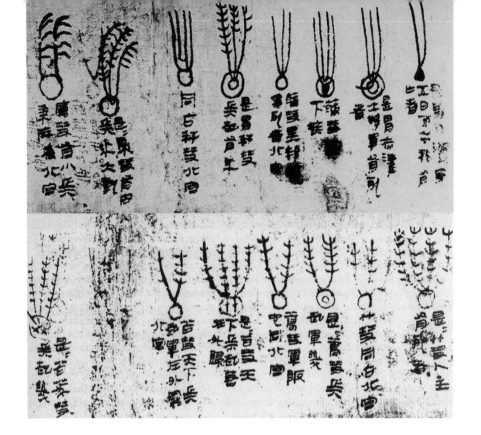

moon Ganymede, over a millennium and a half before Galileo made the same discovery. (Four of the brightest Jovian moons are technically visible to the eye without the aid of a telescope, but usually are hidden in the glare of Jupiter.)

Ominous comets drawn in the ancient Chinese silk manuscript known as the Book of Silk.

While so many texts of antiquity are lost to us, documentary material of Chinese celestial studies has, remarkably, survived the millennia. While the earliest detailed records of scientific *lifa* have been dated to c.100 BC, there are preserved lists of *tianwen* phenomena that go back a further 1000 years. In part, this is due to the fact that they weren't written on paper, but on bone. 'Oracle bones' are animal bones, often from oxen and turtles, heated until cracks were formed, which were then deciphered by fortune tellers, who used them to answer questions ranging from the future weather to the outcomes of military campaigns. Sometimes they were also carved with records of astronomical occurrences. The bones are quite rare, partly because when discovered they were often mistaken for dragon bones which, according to tradition, could be ground up for medicinal purposes. The oracle bone shown above, the oldest object in the collection of the British Library, was etched sometime between 1600 BC and 1050 BC. The writing predicts an absence of bad luck for the coming ten-day period, and on its reverse side carries a record of a lunar eclipse.

A later (though still ancient) Chinese document of note is the manuscript *Divination by Astrological and Meteorological Phenomena*, also known as the *Book of Silk* (shown on page 39). This ancient illustrated astronomical journal, written on silk, was compiled by Chinese astronomers of the Western Han Dynasty (202 BC–AD 9), and only discovered in 1973 in the tombs below the saddle-shaped hills of Mawangdui, south central China. On the pages of this, the first definitive atlas of comets, are detailed twenty-nine of the fiery objects referred to as *huixing* ('broom stars') that were observed in the skies over a period of c.300 years. Each picture is captioned with a corresponding event that it was believed to have heralded, such as 'the death of the prince', 'the coming of the plague' or 'the three-year drought'.

But for the oldest manuscript star atlas of any civilization, we need turn to a document known as the *Dunhuang Star Atlas*. This scroll, more than 6ft (2m) long, was one of 40,000 documents discovered in a hidden cave (now known as the

The Dunhuang paper scroll is the oldest complete preserved star atlas of any civilization. Created in China in AD c.700, centuries before the invention of the telescope, it shows more than 1300 stars visible in the northern hemisphere.

Library Cave) outside the Silk Road town of Dunhuang in northwest China. The atlas is one of the most spectacular documents in the history of astronomy, presenting a complete snapshot of the eighth-century Chinese sky of 1339 stars glimpsed from the imperial observatory (long before the use of telescopes), which continues to surprise modern examiners with its accuracy. Most impressively, the projection (i.e. how a spheroidal sky or planetary surface is drawn on a flat sheet of paper) used by the cartographer is very similar to that created by the sixteenth-century Flemish cartographer Gerardus Mercator, which is still used by mapmakers today. Precious in its own time, that this cosmic marvel survived unmolested for almost a millennium before its modern rediscovery is a fortuity that beggars belief. There is no Western counterpart to such a detailed witness of an early sky.

Zhang Daoling, one of the early Daoist masters of the Eastern Han period, rides through the sky on a celestial tiger, wielding a sword surrounded by the seven stars of the polar constellation of the Big Dipper (Great Bear, Ursa Major).

ANCIENT EGYPTIAN ASTRONOMY

For the ancient Egyptians, whose landscape saw not a drop
of rain for thousands of years, the solstices so essential to other
cultures paled in significance to a peculiar local occurrence:
the annual flooding of the Nile. In mythology it was believed
that the Nile broke its banks each year because it brimmed
with the tears of Isis, the mother goddess of life and healing,
weeping over the death of her husband, Osiris, god of life
and death. In reality the river swelled from the runoff of the
yearly monsoons that brought terrific rainfall to the Ethiopian
Highlands between May and August, an event that rendered
a miraculous irrigational effect (and that continues to be
celebrated by Egyptians as a two-week annual holiday known
as *Wafaa El-Nil*, from 15 August.) The flood cycle was so
reliably consistent that the Egyptians tied it with the equally
regular heliacal rising of the star Sirius, which coincidentally
became visible at the same time.

It was these phenomena that the Egyptians used to
calibrate their administrative calendar of three seasons: Akhet
(inundation, featuring the flooding), Peret (growth) and
Shemu (harvest). Sirius was just one member of the intricate
stellar basis of this calendar, which we know to have been in
use at least as early as the Old Kingdom period (c.2686–2181
BC). The Egyptians identified their own star group known
as the 'decans' – thirty-six small constellations and single
stars – which first appeared on record in the form of coffin-lid
decoration in the Tenth dynasty (c.2100 BC). A new shining
decan would appear heliacally in the sky every ten days, and
so with thirty-six of these appearances the 360-day annual
calendar was formed, with an intercalary month of five days
added for more accurate adjustment. Further detail of these
decans is, however, hard to discern. While their names are
known, and in some cases have been translated ('Hry-ib wiA'
for example has been interpreted as 'in the centre of the ship'
and is associated with Seth, the god of the desert, storms and
violence), exactly which stars they are is unknown, as no
information has survived about their positions, brightness,
how they were selected nor their relationships with other stars.

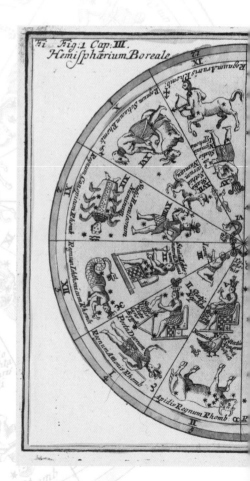

Ancient coffin and tomb decoration do, however, help furnish us with understanding of how the Egyptians incorporated twelve nightly stars into the grand theme of their sky mythology, the nocturnal journey of the falcon-headed solar deity Ra through the Duat, the Egyptian realm of the dead. According to the Amduat ('Book of the Underworld'), Ra travelled west to east aboard his solar vessel. Each night he passed through twelve regions, encountering a host of gods and monsters and battling the giant serpent chaos deity Apep, or Apophis, to emerge with renewed strength as the morning sun. On tables of astronomical data discovered in ancient tombs, referred to today as 'star clocks', we find the twelve stages of Ra's progress through the Underworld Tables represent the twelve hours of the night. With their decanal week also provided, this device allowed the star-literate to tell the time from a quick interpretation of the night sky. (While this has long been the commonly held belief, more recently Sarah

A double-hemisphere celestial chart showing the constellations according to ancient Egyptian astronomers. Published in 1730 by Corbinianus Thomas.

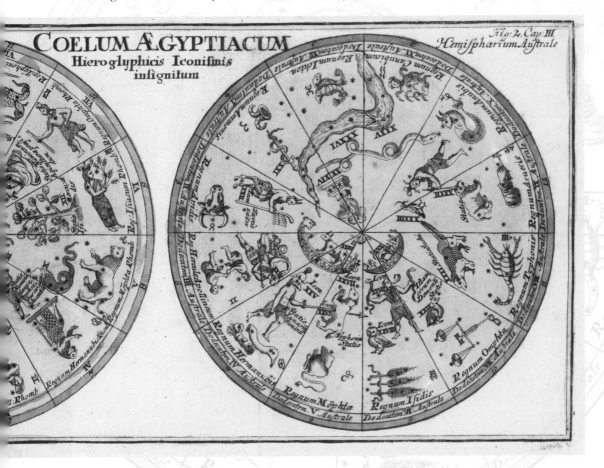

Symons of McMaster University, Ontario and Elizabeth Tasker of Hokkaido University have proposed that the star maps lining the coffins could instead have been installed to help the souls of the dead navigate the night sky, and live eternally in the blazing form of a star.)

ABOVE: *An ancient Egyptian depiction of the Milky Way, which was deified as a fertility cow-goddess by the name of Bat (later combined with the sky-goddess Hathor). Found on the 3000-year-old Djedkhonsuifeankh funerary papyrus.*

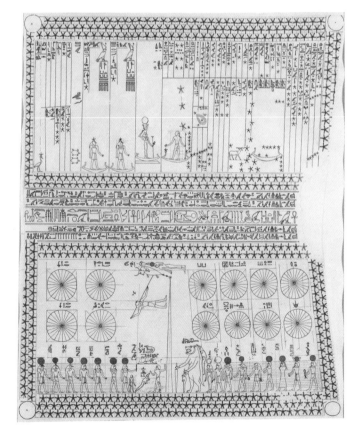

LEFT: *A painting of the celestial diagram adorning the ceiling of the tomb of the Egyptian architect Senenmut (fl. 1473), high steward to Queen Hatshepsut. The star chart shows numerous decans, as well as other personified heavenly bodies.*

The sun-god Ra with the goddess of the West, Amentit, illustrated in burial chamber of Nefertari, wife of Ramses II, c.1298–1235 BC.

North was also significant to Egyptian belief. The Egyptian pyramids have been shown to have knowledge of the stars, and the pole star at the time, Thuban, factored into their construction. It was only in the 1960s that it was realized that the 'air-shafts' built into the Great Pyramid of Giza were not merely ventilation but were aligned with specific stars and areas of the sky. The passages are crooked, so couldn't have been used for observation, but perhaps were to do with the dead pharaoh's ascension to Heaven – it was believed that the constant north was a gateway through which pharaohs travelled to the afterlife. Having noticed that the star Kochab of the Ursa Minor constellation, and another bright star, Mizar of Ursa Major, both seemed to circle the celestial north as if heralding this gateway, the Egyptians nicknamed the duo 'j.ḫmw-sk' (literally 'the ones not knowing destruction' or 'the indestructibles').

Despite this demonstrated role of specific stars in their belief system, in comparison with the wealth of mythological source material there is no evidence of ancient Egyptian star cataloguing, or any other forms of precise recorded

observation. Indeed there is very little to suggest that the ancient Egyptians searched for scientific understanding of the movement of planets and other celestial mechanisms, or treated the sky as anything other than a canvas for mythology and a practical utility for timekeeping. This would change significantly with the merging with Greek and Babylonian astronomy during the Ptolemaic dynasty, which began with the death of Alexander the Great and the accession of his general, Ptolemy I Soter, in 323 BC, and the elevation of Alexandria to the forefront of global scientific activity.

OPPOSITE: *The commemorative Stela of Aafenmut (c.924–889 BC) is topped with Ra's solar barge, with which he navigated the underworld.*

LEFT: *The Dendera Zodiac. Dated to c.50 BC, the bas-relief from the ceiling of a chapel dedicated to Osiris in the Hathor temple at Dendera is the oldest known complete depiction of the classical zodiac. The Babylonian constellations are combined with those of the Egyptians in the centre, while the band of thirty-six figures lining the perimeter represent the decans.*

BELOW: *The astronomical scenes decorating the Tomb of Seti I (1294–1279 BC) feature constellations unlike those of any other classical culture, except the Ox and Handler (centre) recognizable as Ursa Major (the Plough). Elsewhere in the tomb is a depiction for the 'opening of the mouth' ritual, which magically allowed the soul of the departed to eat and drink in the afterlife.*

ABOVE: *The right eye of the sun-god Horus was believed to be the Sun, while his left, shown here in this illustration from the ceiling of the Hathor temple, Dendera, was said to be the Moon. The scene depicted here is symbolic of the waxing Moon; after losing his left eye in a battle with Seth, Horus was healed by Thoth (far right), and over fourteen days the Moon returned to its fullness. The procession of fourteen deities represents each day of this cycle.*

LEFT: *David Robert's 1848 illustration of the temple at Dendera.*

THE ANCIENT GREEKS

The name for our galaxy in English, and indeed many other languages around the world, originates from the ancient Greek myth of Hercules. The goddess Hera agreed to suckle the half-mortal baby, but when he bit down she pushed him away in pain. Her milk spilt out across the sky and formed the Milky Way. While this observation-based mythology is in keeping with that of other ancient cultures, the natural philosophers of ancient Greece, from at least as early as the sixth century BC, differed from their contemporaries by their focus on solving the question of the theoretical structure of the cosmos. What model could rationally explain the movements of the celestial bodies?

The Greek vision of the cosmos, from Le Sphere du Monde, *1549, by Oronce Fine.*

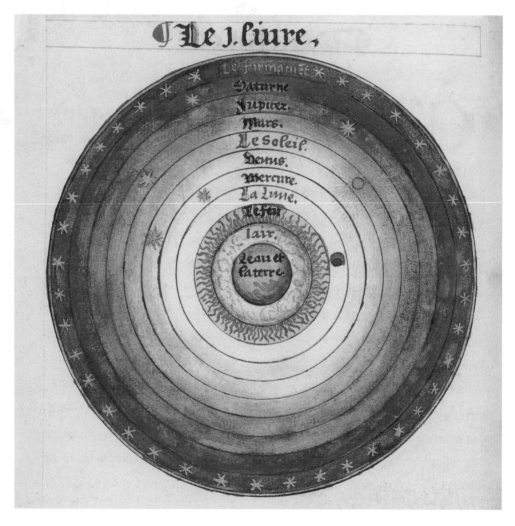

The largest existing part of the Antikythera mechanism, constructed c.150 BC. This complex clockwork mechanism is believed to have been an ancient analogue computer, used to predict astronomical positions and eclipses for calendars. The technology behind the invention was lost, and would not be seen again until the fourteenth century with the appearance of European clockwork.

No celestial maps or theoretical drawings of ancient Greek astronomy have survived, and so to track the early stages of this thinking we start with the cosmic speculation found in the earliest Greek literature. In Homer's *Iliad*, which is believed to have been written sometime around the eighth century BC, we find small but fascinating pieces of information, such as the comparison of Earth to the flat disc of the shield of Achilles, and the description that it is encircled by a huge river, the ocean, the origin of all things including water and 'the Father of all gods'. Homer also makes reference to 'the autumnal star' (Sirius, the brightest in Earth's night sky), as well as to the constellations Hyades and Pleiades (groups that are part of the modern Taurus constellation), Orion, the Bear (Ursa Major, which is 'also called the Wagon') and to the Evening Star and Morning Star, both likely to be Venus. At the end of the night, these heavenly bodies were believed to sink back into the ocean from which they had risen. In the *Odyssey*, the sky is described as a star-filled dome composed of bronze or iron, solid yet unreachable and held up on great pillars. Across this great dome travelled the *ouranodromos* ('sky-running') Helios, god of the Sun.

In the fourth century BC, Aristotle turned a critical lens on the now lost works of earlier thinkers, and through his analysis we learn details of how the four most notable figures of the sixth century – Thales of Miletus, Anaximander, Anaximenes

IN ASTROLOGOS.

and Pythagoras – scrutinized the sky. Thales (c.624–546 BC) was considered by Aristotle to be the founding father of Ionian natural philosophy, and was a figure distinctive for his diversion from mythology in favour of theories based on knowledge of the physical world. Indeed rejecting the 'will of the gods' as a catch-all explanation is the key difference between Ionian and other early cultural approaches to astronomy. For Thales, his knowledge of the heavens was, at times, both a boon and a burden. In one of the earliest examples of a business monopoly, the story goes that Thales used the stars to predict a particularly bounteous harvest season of olives. Having hired every olive press in Miletus and the nearby Aegean island of Chios in anticipation, the scheme made him rich.

A less fortunate incident involved him being so preoccupied with staring up at the stars while walking that he fell straight down a well, to the delight of a watching Thracian slave woman. According to Herodotus in *The Histories*, Thales is the first on record to have made a successful prediction of a solar eclipse, foreseeing the eclipse of 28 May 585 BC, which interrupted a battle between the Medes and the Lydians, and instigated such terror that it swiftly effected a truce. (Because the dates of historical eclipses can be pinpointed accurately by astronomers, Isaac Asimov once described this battle as the earliest historical event dated with precision, and described Thales's prediction as 'the birth of science'.)

Two notable followers of Thales developed his ideas with theories of their own. Anaximander (c.610–546 BC) believed the law of the universe to be geometric, and that this placed Earth at its centre, in equilibrium. He introduced the concept of the *apeiron* ('the boundless'), the cosmological theory that everything originated from an infinite primal chaos, with new worlds created from, and disappearing back into, this hungry eternity. The stars were whirling wheels of air and fire, spitting flame, while Earth itself was a cylinder, with mankind perched atop one flat end. Anaximenes (c.585–528 BC) shared a similar cosmological view, but also developed the idea raised by Thales and propagated by Anaximander of the universe being composed of a grand unifying material. His predecessors had thought this to be water (an idea which we can link back to the aquatic origin mythology described in the Babylonian *Enuma Elish*), but Anaximenes suggested instead that the common material of the universe was air, out of which celestial bodies are condensed.

And then there was Pythagoras (c.570–495 BC). As famous as the name remains, we actually know very little of the man born on the Greek island of Samos. Since at least the first century BC he was credited with the geometric theorem that bears his name (though the idea predates him), a discovery he allegedly marked by sacrificing an ox to the

Though the flat Earth notion had been disproven by Aristotle, the idea lived on in certain quarters of eccentric thought. Take, for example, this map by Professor Orlando Ferguson, printed in 1893. The flat and square Earth is based literally on Revelations 7:1, of there being 'four corners of the Earth'. As for it being stationary, Ferguson includes on the right side a cartoon of men clinging to the speeding planet, scoffing: 'These men are flying on the globe at the rate of 65,000mph [104,600km/h] around the centre of the Earth (in their minds). Think of that speed!'

Pythagoras·

Fabe

Of all the legends involving Pythagoras, perhaps the strangest is his unwavering aversion to beans, represented in this c.1512 French illustration. Supposedly the philosopher forbade his followers from eating the vegetable for fear that the resultant passing of gas was the loss of a piece of one's soul. Unfortunately one night Pythagoras was attacked by an angry mob and chased until reaching a bean field, which he couldn't bring himself to enter. Trapped, his pursuers fell on him with daggers.

gods. The sectarian cult that sprouted from Pythagoras's teachings believed in mathematics as the language of nature, supposedly demonstrated by their founder's observation that a blacksmith struck different 'notes' depending on the size of the hammer he used. Though this is demonstrably false, as hammer size does not affect the note (unlike string length in a piano, for example), what the story serves to represent is the Pythagoreans's concept of numbers being the universal language of the ordered natural world, which exists in harmony with its constituent parts like a living organism. Part of this mathematical philosophy was the recognition of the sphere as the most perfect shape in nature, an ideal form they ascribed to the world and heavens. What exact argument and evidence led them to this conclusion is unknown, but the idea

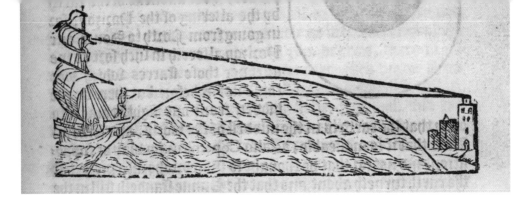

was corroborated by observations of sailors that the visible stars changed as one journeyed north and south, which suggested a curved surface to the world. When Aristotle later presented the lunar eclipse as evidence (see accompanying image) for the sphericity of the world, pointing to the circular shadow cast by the Earth on the lunar surface, the globular Earth was the accepted view of leading thinking. Our widespread modern belief that the prevailing notion at this time was that the Earth was flat is simply not the case.

One clear piece of evidence for a spherical Earth was that, at a distance, the top of a ship comes into view before the rest of it. This concept is illustrated in a wide variety of astronomical texts throughout history (here from M. Blundeuile His Exercises, 1613, by Thomas Blundeville.)

An illustration from Universal Geography *(1711) demonstrating Aristotle's evidence for a lunar eclipse evincing the spherical shape of the Earth (and, for good measure, how it cannot be triangular, square or hexagonal).*

Hoc Schema demonstrat terram esse globosam
This Scheme demonstrates if Earth to be of a Globular form.

p. 30.

Si terra esset trigona, umbra quoque triangulari figura in eclipsi Lunari appareret.
If the Earth were of a Triangular form, if Shadow would appear so in the Eclipse of the Moon.

Si terra esset tetragona umbra quoque tetragone haberet formam.
If the Earth were four square, the Shadow would also be four square.

Si terra hexagone esset figure, ejus quoque umbra in defectu Lunari hexagona appareret, que tamen rotunda.

If the Earth were six-square, if Shadow would be six square in the Eclipse of y Moon which however appears to be round.

THE HEAVENLY SPHERES

To explain the universe, the Greeks took the round Earth and made a logical extrapolation – that the heavens were also of a spherical nature. 'The creator fashioned the world a rounded, spherical shape', notes Plato, '… and he established a single, spherical universe in circular motion.' Aristotle, who joined Plato's academy in Athens as a teenager and remained until the age of thirty-seven, shared in the idea of the spherical universe. Just as modern astronomers would later have to establish the boundary of 'Outer Space', Aristotle tackled the question of

A map by Cellarius that attempts to show the orbits of the planets in three dimensions. The Greeks believed these movements indicated the existence of physical spheres carrying the celestial bodies. The traditional flat depiction of the Ptolemaic system is in the bottom-left corner, and Tycho Brahe's idea in the bottom right.

Aristotle's four elements,
from the encyclopaedic work
De proprietatibus rerum
('The Properties of Things') by
Bartholomaeus Anglicus, 1491.

where the sky began. He drew a dividing line between the disorder and impermanence of the terrestrial plane with its four basic elements, and the perfect geometry of the celestial realm, which was, he theorized, composed of a 'quintessence', a fifth element known as ether. Any erratic anomalies spotted in the sky were explained with terrestrial association: comets, for example, were an event local to the upper atmosphere, where earthly exhalations burst into flame. This, writes Aristotle in *Meteorology*, was also the explanation for optical phenomena like the Aurora Borealis and for the Milky Way.

Plato bid his contemporaries decode the patterns of the planetary motions, a challenge that was taken up by Eudoxus of Cnidus (c.400–347 BC), a younger contemporary mathematician. Eudoxus broke apart the problematic variety of planetary movements with a simple solution: he added more spheres, nested inside each other. He assigned to each of the five known planets four spinning spheres made of ether, each influencing a different planetary direction, to explain the puzzle of retrograde (backward) movement, and both daily and annual changes in position. The Sun and Moon were each given three ethereal spheres, while the largest one carried all the stars. In all, Eudoxus's sky consisted of twenty-seven concentric spheres. To help clarify the essence of this spherical concept, imagine a transparent crystal ball within which is another slightly smaller transparent crystal ball containing an even smaller crystal sphere, and so on. This set of crystal spheres, packed within each other like a set of Russian

matryoshka ('nesting dolls') were each thought to physically carry a celestial body on their shell, with the larger outside spheres carrying the planets farther from Earth. At the centre of this glass machine of rotating spherical layers lay Earth, with Man looking up and out at this rotating cosmic machination.

This extraordinary spherical vision of the cosmic architecture would enjoy remarkable longevity, fortified by the endorsement of Aristotle, who expanded the number of spheres to fifty-five. In line with his conviction that anything in perpetual motion must be perpetually caused to move, he credited the grand scheme of all celestial movement to a mysterious *primum movens* ('prime mover'), an ultimate unseen force that would later, of course, fit perfectly with the God of Christianity.

Eudoxus's original writing is lost, but survives in adapted form thanks to the Greek didactic poet Aratus of Soli, who between 276 BC and 274 BC rewrote the prose in 732 verses of hexameter to form the wildly popular astronomical poem *Phaenomena*, a work so significant that it was translated into Latin and Arabic (one of only a few early Greek poems to enjoy this cultural crossing), and continued to be reproduced well into the medieval period. (It can even be found quoted in the New Testament by the apostle Paul in Acts 17, following his journey to Athens.) The *Phaenomena* introduces and describes the constellations and lays out the rules for the risings and settings of each star grouping, allowing its reader to tell the time at night. It also details the structure of Eudoxus's spheres,

FOLLOWING PAGES: *The constellations Sagittarius and Capricorn, the stars marked in orange. Taken from a manuscript produced in the mid-eleventh century (just before the Norman Conquest of England) of Cicero's* Aratea, *a poetic translation of Aratus's* Phaenomena.

the path of the Sun in the zodiac and how to predict the weather. Aratus was no scientist though, asserting in the initial lines of the poem that, ultimately, all things are entirely the work of Zeus. Perhaps it is this softening of astronomical data with mythological allusions and literary charm that gives the work its appeal, and helps account for its widespread popularity.

The *Phaenomena* was not without errors, and indeed the sole surviving text of the great astronomical observer Hipparchus (162–127 BC), considered the founder of trigonometry, is his *Commentary on the Phaenomena of Aratus and Eudoxus*, pointing out the astronomical errors and criticizing the descriptions of the constellations provided by both Aratus and Eudoxus. Listing the achievements of Hipparchus helps give some sense of the profound transformation Greek astronomy was undergoing at this time, as the influence of older observational Babylonian methodologies were absorbed. Apparently motivated by a suspicion that a star had inexplicably moved position, in 129 BC Hipparchus assembled the first comprehensive star catalogue of the Western skies, to ensure future generations were equipped to test any other such migrations. By ranking the stars in six tiers by order of brightness, he invented the first stellar magnitude scale – a system still used in modern astronomy though, of course, in much more precise form.

As well as discovering a nova, it was Hipparchus who is usually credited as inventing the first reliable method for predicting solar eclipses and who devised the earliest surviving quantitative models for the motions of the Sun and Moon, drawing on the mathematical techniques and astronomical records of the Babylonians. His most famous discovery, however, was the precession of the equinoxes (today more commonly referred to as axial precession), the gradual rotation of the heavens observable to the earthbound sky-watcher, in a cycle that spans a period of approximately 25,772 years. Hipparchus estimated the turning of the starry sphere to move at a rate of one degree in a century – the actual number is one degree per seventy-two years, but this hardly detracts from such an impressive early discovery.

To add to his achievements, Eudoxus is believed by scholars to have created the first celestial globe, though it has not survived. It's thought that the Farnese Atlas shown here, the oldest celestial globe in existence, carried on the back of the Titan of Greek mythology, was directly influenced by Eudoxus's work, as well as that of the second-century BC astronomer Hipparchus.

FABULA CAPRICORNUS

CAPRICORNUS huius effigies similis est aegipani que iuppit et quod cum eo erat
nutritus insidentis esse uoluit aut capram nutricem de qua ante diximus Hic etia dr
cu iuppit graias ob pugnaret prim obiecisse eum hostib: amore qui
panicos uocatur utera ostenes dic hac etiam decausa eius inferiore
parte piscis ee deformat maxam qd muricib: hostis sit idculatus plapidum
iactione capricor nus occesum dspectans et totus inodiaco circulo
deformat edude ed toto corpore medius diuidit adhiemali circulo sub
posit aquaru indua simi stra occidit pceps exort dui direct et habet
innaso stella una infra ceruices und inpectore
duas inprima pede una inposteriori pede
altam inscaplio vii inuentre v incauda iii
omnino stella rum xxvi

Corpore semifero magno capricornus inorbe
Queincam ppecuo uestiuit lumine titan
Brumali flectens contorquet tempore currum
Hoc caduete inpontum studeas committere mense
Iam non longincum spdtium habere diurnum
Non hiberna cito uoluetur curriculo nox
Humida non se se uris durora querellis
Oaus ostendit dari prenuntia solis
At ualidis equor pulsabit uirib: duster
Tum fissum tremulo quatietur frigore corpus
Sedtamen dinuiam labuntur tempore toto
Hetui signoru cedunt neque flammia uitant
Hec metuunt canos minitantia murmure fluctus

CAPRICORNUS

P manus ex meatus signi regione rodicatur circulus humillimus e. ppa
requino serma. Quidam negant dicentes. Numquam centauros sagittarius
asas fuisse. Sosithe us dutem illum adhirunt filium illu musarum tale se
ha bet stellas incapite in meacumine sagittae in in
cubito in manu i. inuentore i. clarum indorso n
incauda i. ingenu priori i. insummo pede i.
in posteriori genu i fiunt xun.

A tque decidm sup hoc ndui pelagoq: ua gatur
M ense sagitti potens solis cusustu net orbem
H dm idm cumminus exiguo lux tempore presto est
h oc signu ueniens poterunt prenoscere ndute
l dm ppe peipitante licebit uisere nocte
u t se se ostendens ostendat scorpius dlte
p osteriore trahens flexum in corporis drtum
l dm sup hunc cernes dru cdpat esse minoris
E t magis erectu adsummu uersarier orbem
l um se se orion toto idm corpore condet
E xtrema ppe nocte etcepheus conditor dlte
l umboru tenus dprima depulsus dsumbras.

SAGITTARIUS

THE PTOLEMAIC COSMOS

Claudius Ptolemy, pointing to the stars.

Three hundred years later, following a period considered something of a dark age in astronomical scholarship, we at last find firmer documentary footing with the work of the mathematician, geographer and astronomer Claudius Ptolemy (AD c.100–170). Through his writing we learn that the Alexandrian scholar greatly admired Hipparchus as a 'lover of truth' and his most significant predecessor. In his magnificent astronomical work known as the *Almagest* (AD c.150), Ptolemy incorporated, unaltered, the Nicaean's model of the Sun's movement, featuring his original calculation that Earth had to be in an eccentric, or off-centre, position within its circular path to account for the variation in the length of the seasons. Ptolemy also expanded Hipparchus's star catalogue from 850 to 1022 stars, applying coordinates and including the visible nebulae. His forty-eight constellations would be the authoritative foundation of astronomy for more than

The UNIVERSE after COSMAS 550.

1000 years, until the early seventeenth century. The pinnacle of centuries of observation and cosmic understanding, the *Almagest* successfully provided geometric models to predict – with an impressive level of accuracy – the movements of the planetary wanderers, tables that would be of great use to mathematical astronomers and astrologers.

Though Ptolemy does not lay out his own complete system of the cosmos as his predecessors had done, we can conjure a picture of the Ptolemaic universe* by combining his ordering of the planetary spheres, based on their heights above Earth, and his calculations in a later work called *Planetary Hypotheses*. In this Ptolemy calculates the distance of the planets from Earth, and so we get the first attempts to mathematically measure the size of the universe, using as a cosmic unit Earth's radius, which he thought to be roughly 5000 miles (8500km). Thus he suggests Earth is c.300,000 miles (480,000km) from the Moon (in reality it is on average 238,900 miles/384,500km) and

Cosmas Indicopleustes (literally 'Cosmas who sailed to India') was a Greek merchant and then hermit from Alexandria (home of Ptolemy), who died AD c.550. Cosmas drew many maps based on his travels and Christian beliefs, including this theoretical idea of the universe taking the form of a giant box with a curved lid based on the tabernacle, the earthly dwelling of God.

*Despite the fact that Ptolemy's calculations form the basis of both celestial and terrestrial coordinative mapping, not a single diagram, globe or orrery of his has survived. Though there is no indication that examples ever, in fact, existed, it is hard to imagine the idea to do so eluding Ptolemy or his contemporaries.

5 million miles (8 million km) from the Sun (actually around 92 million miles/148 million km). In keeping with Eudoxus's theory of nested spheres, the starry sphere was the farthest, at c.100 million miles (160 million km) away – the radius of the universe.

This means that the diameter of the spherical Ptolemaic cosmos was c.200,000 million miles (320,000 million km). This figure might seem of rather humble proportions to the modern sky-watcher (Saturn, when at its closest point to Earth, is c.746 million miles/1200 million km away), but it would have been of an astounding vastness to the pre-Copernican, while, at the same time, establishing the Heavens as a finite and geometrically ordered realm. It would not be for at least another 1300 years, until the Copernican revolution in the sixteenth century, that this Ptolemaic model of Earth at the centre of a set of nested spheres would be challenged.

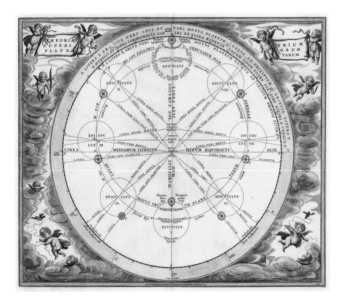

ABOVE: *Cellarius's map illustrating the ancient idea of epicycles (small circles). In the Ptolemaic model, to explain why the orbits of the planets and the Moon didn't fit a perfectly circular path, epicycles were proposed, themselves travelling around Earth on larger circles called deferents.*

RIGHT: Planisphaerium Ptolemaicum… *by Andreas Cellarius, 1661, showing the Ptolemaic geocentric model with the planets as gods racing around their orbits in chariots.*

SEV CAPRICORNVS ♑ ZO SAGITTARIVS ♐

PTOLEMAICVM,
Machina
EX HYPOTHESI
ICA IN PLA·
SPOSITA.

DIA

SCORPIVS ♏

VIA

CIRCVLVS

SOLIS

CIRCVLVS MARTIS

SEPTEM

CVS. LIBRA

ORBIS LVNE

MVNDVS SVBLVNARIS QVATVOR ELEMENTA COMPLECTENS.

NE

TARVM

ITER MER

CVRII

ORBES

☿ ☿ ♀ ♂ ♃ ♄

♍ VIRGO

SATVRNI

♌ LEO

♊ GEMINI

♋ CANCER

THE JAIN UNIVERSE

OPPOSITE: *From the fourth century BC, elements of Greek, Babylonian, Byzantine and Roman astronomy spread to India, causing a shift to observational cosmology away from traditions such as that illustrated in this Jain map of the universe, c.1850. The ancient Indian religion of Jainism developed in the Ganges basin around the seventh and sixth centuries BC, with a cosmology that was outstandingly complex – and in some aspects, advanced – among ancient religions. For the Jain, the universe is an infinite system with no overseeing deity, taking a form akin to a narrow-waisted man with arms and legs outstretched. It is made of six substances: jīva ('souls'), pudgala ('non-sentient matter'), dharma ('motion'), adharma ('the principle of rest'), ākāśa ('space') and kāla ('time'). Jain cosmological maps such as these portrayed this idea of the universe, with a celestial realm at the top, and the infernal netherworld below the terrestrial realm. Today it's estimated that there are more than 7 million followers of the Jain religion – including Vikram Sarabhai (founder of the Indian space programme) and Seth Walchand Hirachand (founder of HAL, Asia's largest aerospace company).*

LEFT: *The universe in the traditional Jain form of a wide-armed man, from the seventeenth-century text* Saṁgrahaṇīratna *by Śrīcandra.*

In the timeline of Western astronomy, the centuries following the appearance of Ptolemy's *Almagest* in the second century AD is a period of marked decline. The cultural golden age of Athens had long since wilted, and no great astronomer had risen to rival the success of Ptolemaic science. Irreparable cracks, meanwhile, were spreading through the soon-to-fall Roman Empire, as Europe headed towards the Early Middle Ages.

Historically this period has been labelled the Dark Ages, but this is a problematic term that modern medievalists spend a good deal of their time wearily debunking. The idea of a developmentally stagnant era was originated by the fourteenth-century Roman poet Petrarch, biased in his portrayal of a period deprived of the shining domination of Rome. The actual phrase 'dark ages' is derived from the Latin term *saeculum obscurum*, created c.1602 by the Roman Catholic cardinal Caesar Baronius. Significantly Baronius used the term to refer specifically to the lack of source material from the tenth and eleventh centuries, not as a pejorative label for the era as a whole, and indeed he marks the end of his 'dark ages' with the Gregorian reforms of 1046, from which point the survival rate of documentary evidence vastly increases.

The dearth of surviving contemporary texts obscures much of this period to modern historians, but the key works of antiquity endured thanks to an elaborate intercultural transmission system. After the fall of Rome, many Greek texts and the science they contained found their way to the libraries of Byzantium, the Greek colony that would come to be known as Constantinople in the fourth century under the Roman emperor Constantine I. None of these reading spaces exist today, but they were reportedly exquisite havens of scholarship. The library built by the patriarch Sergios I in the seventh century, for example, was described by a contemporary poet as 'a spiritual meadow that fills the earth with sweet smells for the soul'.

FOLLOWING PAGES: Asgårdsreien *(1872) by Peter Nicolai Arbo. This giant painting depicts the Norse myth of the Wild Hunt, a cavalcade of Norse gods and the souls of the dead charging across the sky in a midwinter campaign of terror. The motif spread throughout European folklore, igniting imaginations whenever the rumble of thunder was heard.*

EVAL SKY

'I remember giants born early in time, long ago;
I remember nine worlds.'

Prophecy of the Seeress, from the fourteenth-century Icelandic *Hauksbók*

(Sadly the 'meadow' burnt down twice, in 726 and 790.) But it was farther east that these works were drawn most hungrily for their new theories and methodologies, to contribute to a scientific development that would greatly outshine that of Early Middle Ages Europe, an eruption of invention that defined the cultural flourishing of the Islamic Golden Age from the eighth to the fourteenth century.

The ancient Greek idea of the celestial spheres integrated with Christian notions, with angels falling from grace to become the devils of Hell. From the Neville of Hornby Hours *manuscript, created c.1325-1375.*

THE RISE OF ISLAMIC ASTRONOMY

In 641, the Islamic forces of the caliph overwhelmed the fortifications of the Egyptian port city of Alexandria and seized control. In the following years, despite the change in management, the city continued to function largely as it had under Byzantine rule – Greek, Coptic and Arabic were spoken fluently throughout, and the study of medicine, mathematics and alchemy continued apace in what had long been a city of learning. At a time of growing Islamic intellectualism, the Arabs readily adopted the guardianship of this centre of scholarship, and its material legacy.

The value of Greek and other Western scientific texts had been recognized long before the birth of the prophet Muhammad at Mecca c.570. In the fourth century, translations had been made at the School of Edessa (now the Turkish city of Urfa), one of the world's first universities, under the Christian St Ephrem the Syrian. When the school was closed in 489, a number of its faculty moved to Gondishapur, Iran, where for centuries they continued translating Greek works into Syriac. Following the death of the prophet Muhammad, Islam spread like wildfire to north Africa, Spain and Portugal with the Umayyad conquest of Hispania. In 762 the Abbasid Caliphate, the third Islamic caliphate to succeed the prophet Muhammad, founded a new capital city on the west bank of the Tigris – Baghdad – which by the tenth century would be the largest city in the world. This brought the Abbasid court, with its desire to further enrich its culture from classical sources, within proximity of the Christian academics of Gondishapur. This contact facilitated the accumulation of antiquity's great intellectual jewels from Greece, Persia, Egypt and India. With the founding of the Abbasid academy known as the House of Wisdom in the ninth century, these works entered the Arabic language thanks to the industry of Greek- and Syriac-speaking translators. Soon, and rather unexpectedly, through this Islamic religious network Arabic became the international language of science.

About 10,000 astronomical manuscripts – an enormous body of literature – written in Arabic, Persian or Turkish has survived from the medieval era. While many of these

OPPOSITE: *The fresco painting from the ruins of Qasr Amra, a desert castle in present-day Jordan built in 723–743 for the Umayyad caliph Walid II. This is believed to be the earliest surviving painting of the night sky on a non-flat surface. The constellations of the classical zodiac are just about discernible, painted facing in an anti-clockwise direction, their positions as if viewed from outside the celestial sphere. This matches the Farnese Atlas globe (see page 59) and indicates the influence of outside classical sources on this distinctly Islamic creation.*

works have, over the centuries, been left to a quiet shelf life
in collections around the world, ongoing digitization projects
such as that of the British Library help provide further
examples of the issues faced by Islamic astronomers of the
ninth century and beyond. The principal challenge was how
to reconcile new science with the teachings of the prophet

Muhammad, especially when it came to the Islamic calendar. Unlike other cultures, the Islamic, or *Hijri*, calendar was – and continues to be – lunar-based, with a year consisting of 354 or 355 days. In the time before Islam, there is evidence to suggest that, in Central Arabia, this was adjusted for synchronization with the seasons by adding an intercalary month, but after the time of the prophet Muhammad this intercalation was forbidden. (With the year shorn of eleven to twelve days, this means that Islamic calendar events such as Ramadan continue to move around, occurring at any time of year.) Traditionally the beginning of each month was established not through calculation but sky-watching, when the lunar crescent was first spotted in the night sky. Weather was an obvious hindrance to this technique, with towns beginning their calendar at different times, depending on which experienced cloudy skies. Astronomers were also faced with the problem of how to work out the five times of daily prayer with precision; and then there was the challenge of identifying the *kiblah*, the direction to face the *Kaaba*, the sacred shrine at Mecca, when praying.*

To equip those attempting to resolve these difficulties, the *zij* was created. *Zijes* are astronomical handbooks filled with tables of data drawn from that provided by Ptolemy's *Almagest*, as well as other Greek and Indian sources. One could consult a *zij* to calculate the celestial position of the Sun, Moon, stars and planets and find suggestions as to when their first appearances of each month might occur. The *zijes* were limited in accuracy to one latitude, and often had to be recalibrated with updated data to compensate for the precession of the equinoxes (which to the earthbound observer had the effect of the stars gradually shifting position). The sheer number of *zijes* produced shows just how vital the science of astronomy was in the eighth and ninth centuries. In his book *Explanation of Zijes*, the ninth-century Muslim astronomer Al-Hashimi demonstrates the delicate balance astronomers needed to maintain between science and religion, playing down the supernatural 'soothsaying' aspect of the *zij* based on Indian information – presumably in the knowledge of how un-Islamic this would be, for the Koran states that nobody but God can see the future. (Their mathematical derivability, argued Al-Hashimi, renders them safe to draw from.)

*Today, worshippers only have to consult GPS-powered apps such as Google's 'Qibla Finder'.

INVENTING THE STAR-TAKER

Ptolemy's texts and their advanced planetary models provided Islamic astronomers of the Early Modern era with revolutionary geometric computations, but their effectiveness hinged on the figures he provided, and these were decidedly out of date. An advanced method of celestial data-harvesting was called for, a revolution of fresh observation using Ptolemaic techniques to create a new record (and, ultimately, a mapping) of the sky with unprecedented clarity).

Islamic astronomers met this challenge with the astrolabe ('star-taker'), the most important practical tool of medieval astronomy. These handheld astronomical devices, used to measure the inclined positions of celestial bodies among many other things, are of ancient origin, certainly known to Ptolemy, and shown to have been in use at least as early as 150 BC. (The earliest surviving dated astrolabe was crafted much later, by the tenth-century Islamic maker Nastulus – see accompanying image.)

Muslim astronomers developed the astrolabe into a formidable computational device, adding angular scales and indicators for the azimuth (the arc of the horizon measured clockwise from the south point), and used it to find the times of the risings of the Sun and fixed stars, as well as aiding in the scheduling of *salat* ('morning prayers') and determining the *kiblah*. The instrument is essentially a brass disc with a second intricately carved rotating brass plate known as the rete (literally 'net') pinned to its surface. The key to understanding the complexity

The earliest dated Islamic astrolabe, used for astronomical measurements. An inscription on the cast-bronze instrument gives its maker's name as Muhammad ibn Abdallah, known as Nastulus, and the date of its creation which corresponds to 927–928.

of this fascia is simply adopting the right perspective. If we lay the device flat, facing upwards, and look down on it, in the concept of the device we the observer are positioned at the celestial North Pole, the top of the celestial sphere, looking down at the stars of the northern skies spread out flat on the plane of the device. (The southern skies, conceptually 'hidden' on the other side, were not observable to Arab and European users of the device, and so were unnecessary.) The face of the device is, essentially, a two-dimensional map of the three-dimensional sky, the various engraved markers of the rete indicating the positions of the most visible stars. Later Western inventors increased its facility by turning it into a twenty-four-hour clock, with twenty-four markings around the outer edge. By aligning the central index bar with the Sun's position on the ecliptic – its path of movement against the backdrop of the seemingly fixed-position stars – the bar functions like the hands of a clock.

On the reverse side of the astrolabe can be found details of the Sun on the ecliptic and in the centre another moving part – the observing bar known as the alidade ('index bar'), pinned in place. The user holds the device up to the sky by its brass ring so that it hangs vertically, and rotates the alidade until it matches the altitude of the celestial body being observed. Using the scale engraved on the disc, he or she can then note the corresponding angle. When used with a star catalogue, the position and movement of hundreds of stars can be calculated. Such a powerful yet simple tool was not only essential to Islamic and Christian astronomers of the Middle Ages but also fundamental to astrology and astrology-based medicine.

LEFT AND BELOW: The face of an astrolabe with the rete clipped to its surface; and on the reverse the alidade and various notched rules of measurement.

OPPOSITE: The Mogul emperor Jahangir holding what is likely a celestial globe by the great craftsman Muhammad Saleh Thattvi, c.1617.

ISLAMIC CELESTIAL WORKS REACH EUROPE

With the medieval Islamic astronomer armed with the astrolabe, celestial globe, armillary sphere (a model of the celestial globe built from rings and hoops), and the firm footing of Ptolemaic instruction, a new generation were primed to build on the science with their own observations. Observatories were constructed to house instruments of increasingly great size, but these structures were often short-lived. In 1125 in Cairo, for example, the local vizier of the Fatimid caliph was charged with communicating with the planet Saturn and, therefore, executed. An observatory under construction nearby was also destroyed, and its astronomers chased away. Another observatory built later by Sultan Murad III in Istanbul in 1577 (finished at around the same time as the first to be built in northern Europe by Tycho Brahe – see Tycho Brahe entry on page 124) also lasted only a few years, after local religious figures convinced the sultan to demolish it in 1580 to avoid the holy wrath incurred by spying on the heavens.

While observatories suffered a low survival rate, the great and elegant written works of Islamic astronomy fared considerably better. Many of these works would filter through to Western Europe by way of Muslim Spain,

Opposite: The angel Ruh of Islamic belief holds the celestial spheres, from a manuscript created in western Iran in the second half of the 1500s.

The Sun as a king on his wheeled chariot, rolling though his domain. From Albumasar's De magnis conjunctionibus, *1489. The text was one of the earliest vehicles for the transmission of Aristotelian concepts to the West.*

A celestial dragon from al-Qazwini's The Wonders of Creation, c.1280.

A celestial dragon from al-Qazwini's The Wonders of Creation, *c.1280.*

introducing not only Islamic astronomy but also its classical Greek and Indian sources. For example, one of the earliest of these manuscript works was the *Zij al-Sindh* (830) of Muhammad ibn Mūsā al-Khwārizmī, chief librarian at the Baghdad House of Wisdom, and whose name is, incidentally, the origin of the word 'algorithm'. Based on Hindu texts, the work was translated into Latin in the twelfth century by Adelard of Bath, and so its Indian science entered European circulation. The *zij* of the Syrian astronomer Al-Battani (c.858–929), who made the remarkable determination of the solar year as being 365 days, 5 hours, 46 minutes and 24 seconds (which is only 2 minutes and 22 seconds off), was another greatly influential work in Europe. Copernicus quotes Al-Battani twenty-three times in his seminal *De revolutionibus orbium coelestium* of 1543 (see The Copernican Revolution entry on page 120), and Tycho Brahe, Giovanni Battista Riccioli and others also make admiring references to his work.

Another famous name is that of Abu Ma'shar (787–886), better known to Europeans as Albumasar. The native of Khorasan, Persia, was an astrologer, the greatest of the Abbasid

Representation of the
Moon also from The
Wonders of Creation
*by Zakariya al-
Qazwini (1203–1283),
an important Arabic
cosmographical work.
The colourful work was
designed to entertain
as much as it was to
inform. Completed
c.1280, the book explores
the Islamic idea of there
being two universes:
Aalam-ul-Ghaib ('the
unseen universe'), which
is invisible to man, and
home to Allah, angels,
Paradise, Hell, the seven
heavens and Al-Arsh
('the Divine Throne');
and Alam-ul-Shahood
('the observable
universe'), perceptible
to the five senses.*

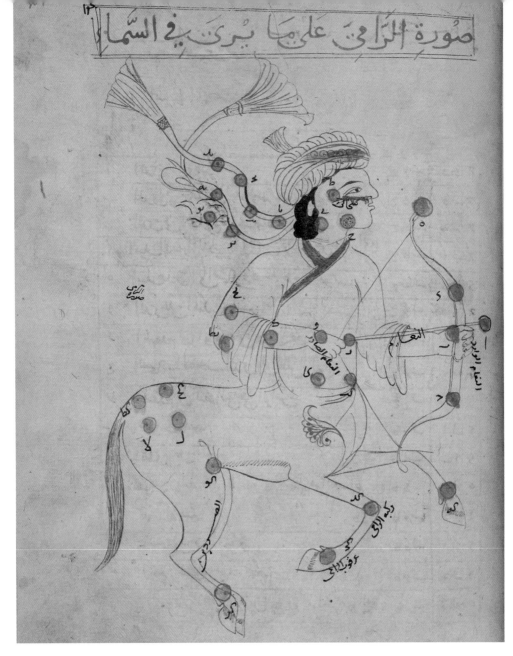

صورة الرامي على ما يرى في السما

court in Baghdad. It was a profession that carried some risk, as Albumasar found out when he correctly predicted a celestial event and for his trouble was ordered to be whipped by the caliph al-Musta'in. 'I hit the mark and I was severely punished,' Albumasar grumbled. After a public dispute with the leading philosopher Abu Yūsuf al-Kindi, Albumasar spent years training in mathematics, astronomy and Platonic and Aristotelian philosophy in order to better defend the validity of his art. Though his original manuscripts are no longer extant, many of his astrological manuals, centred around his argument that the entirety of past and future human events are dictated

ABOVE AND OPPOSITE:
Illustrations from the Book on the Constellations of Fixed Stars *by Abd al-Rahman al-Sufi, an astronomical text written c.964. Writing in Arabic, the Persian author al-Sufi synthesizes Ptolemy's comprehensive star catalogues in the* Almagest *with the traditional Arabic constellations.*

by the positions of the planets, were pored over by astrologers in Muslim and Christian traditions throughout the Middle Ages.

While Al-Battani had made corrections to Ptolemy's work, the first to truly overhaul the *Almagest* was Abd al-Rahman al-Sufi (903–986), with his *Book on the Constellations of Fixed Stars* c.964. With enhanced magnitudes and recalculated longitudes to account for the precession of the equinoxes, sl-Sufi's manuscript sets out to relate the Greek constellations with their traditional Arabic names, and for clarity lays out each constellation with two illustrations: one depicts it from the viewpoint of an observer outside the celestial; the other from within. Beautiful and evocative, the *Book... of Fixed Stars* is laden with wonders for the modern astronomical historian to pick through. Al-Sufi presents the earliest known descriptions and depictions of what he called 'a little cloud', which is actually the Andromeda Galaxy; and also the first description of the Large Magellanic Cloud, a satellite galaxy of the Milky Way c.163,000 light years away. It's also thought that his cataloguing of a specific 'nebulous star' in the southern sky refers to Omicron Velorum, a bright star cluster in the constellation Vela; and his observation of a 'nebulous object' in the faint Vulpecula constellation is a cluster that today is known as al-Sufi's Cluster, or the 'Coat hanger asterism'. All of this achieved, remember, far before the invention of the telescope.

FOLLOWING PAGES: *The exquisite horoscope made for Sultan Jalāl al-Dīn Iskandar Sultan ibn Umar Shaykh, grandson of Tamerlane, the Turkman Mongol conqueror. Drawn in 1411, in the form of a planisphere, it shows the position of the planets at the moment of Iskandar Sultan's birth on 25 April 1384. The lavish gilt detail captures the astrologer's prediction of a long and successful life.*

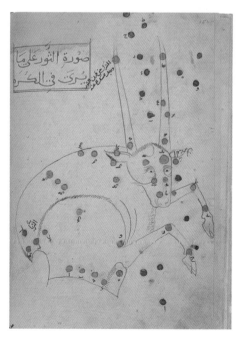

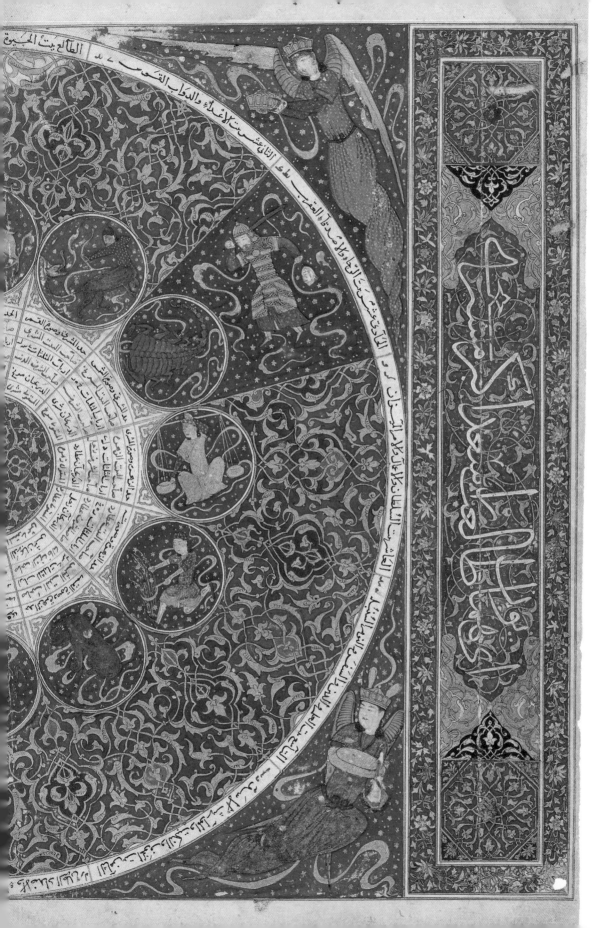

EUROPEAN ASTRONOMY

While Arabic science flourished in the early medieval era, in part catalyzed by the rich discovery of Ptolemaic and other Greek and scientific Indian texts, in Europe this intellectual heritage would not meet Western eyes until at least the tenth century, when European scholars such as Gerbert of Aurillac (later to be known as Pope Sylvester II) chased rumours of Arabic learning to Spain and Sicily. In the field of astronomy, the landmark translation of Ptolemy's *Almagest* by Gerard of Cremona (c.1114–1187) from Arabic texts found in Toledo, would not take place until the twelfth century.

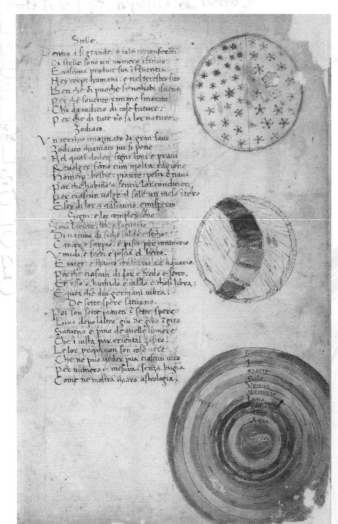

Planets of the mid-14th century, from a manuscript by the Italian friar and humanist Leonardo de Piero Dati.

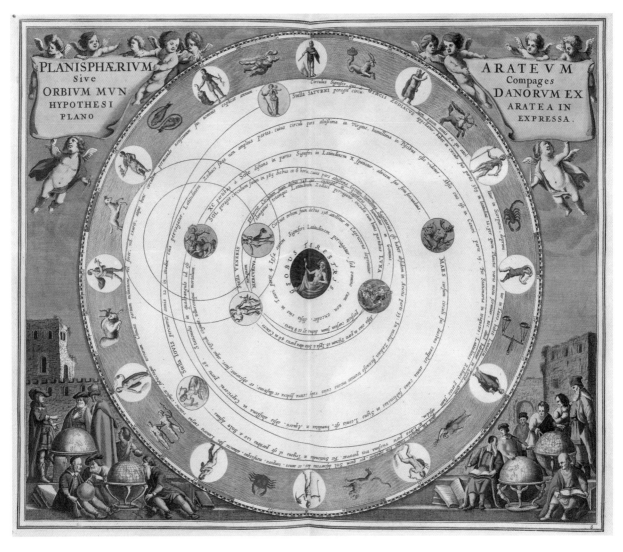

Just as the rise of Islam had for Arabic scientists both facilitated and freighted astronomers with the task of developing knowledge in harmony with a prescribed religious framework, so the thinkers of Western Europe sought to develop a cosmographical picture congruous with the teachings of the Christian Church. Following the breaking apart of the Roman Empire in the second half of the fifth century, and the dissolution of the relative tranquillity throughout the Mediterranean world known as the *pax romana*, Christianity had risen to fill the structural vacuum. Much of Greek science had been lost, and lacking the wealth of classical sources available to their Islamic counterparts Europeans initially turned to the materials of the ruling authority, the

Cellarius maps the cosmic system of Martianus Capella (mistakenly attributing it to Aratus).

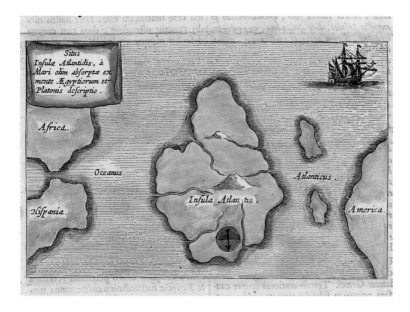

Athanasius Kircher's map of Atlantis. The legend is one of the many allegorical curiosities described in Plato's dialogue Timaeus.

biblical scriptures. The cosmovision of the first millennium AD was built not from rational observation but dogmatic interpretation. To the compulsively curious, though, it was evident that biblical pronunciations left questions unanswered, and a few surviving works of antiquity translated from Greek to Latin would be a vital recourse for the secular student. Two-thirds of Plato's cosmological myth *Timaeus* survived thanks to Calcidius of the fourth century. The work is mostly a dialogue between Athenian figures including Socrates, Timaeus, Hermocrates and Critias, who discuss the nature of the physical world, the purpose and properties of the universe, and the creation of the World Soul, a compound of Being, Sameness and Difference. (Calcidius's translation and detailed commentary would be popular well into the late Middle Ages.)

Another of the more famous Latin works that heavily informed the mind of the Early Middle Ages astronomer was *De nuptiis philologiae et mercurii* ('On the Marriage of Philology and Mercury') by Martianus Capella (c.365–440) of Carthage, a didactic allegory that uses the 'plot' of Mercury and Philology united in marriage through the efforts of Apollo, and forms an encyclopedic source of information about the Roman liberal arts. The work was influential in establishing the early medieval structure of academic learning, based around the seven liberal arts: grammar, rhetoric and logic (the *trivium*) – and geometry, arithmetic, music and astronomy (the *quadrivium*). One of Capella's more prominent astronomical

Opposite: The frontispiece illumination from a fifteenth-century Italian manuscript of Macrobius's commentary on Cicero's Somnium scipionis, *showing Cicero and his dream of the starry universe.*

statements in the book, repeated into the time of Copernicus, who notes it with some perplexity, is that Venus and Mercury closely circled the Sun, while the three together circled Earth, an idea that dates back to Heraclides of Pontus (390–310 BC). Meanwhile cosmological ideas derived from the works of Plato and Cicero, and the Pythagoreans' concept of mathematics underpinning the universe, were provided by Macrobius Ambrosius Theodosius, a Roman provincial in the early fifth century. Macrobius's *Commentarii in somnium scipionis* ('Commentary on the Dream of Scipio') was one of the most widely read sources of Platonism in the Latin West through the Middle Ages, and lays out the structure of the cosmos: seven spherical planets circling a spherical Earth (itself divided into four inhabited quarters by ocean) at the centre of a spherical universe, encased by a starry sphere that pulled the planets along on their path with its slow rotation.

As it had been for Islamic astronomers, in Christendom a balance was struck with the Church through the help astronomy offered with several practical problems faced by the pious. The sixth-century Bishop Gregory of Tours mentions that he learnt his astronomy from the works of Capella, and describes a method by which monks could determine the time of prayer at night by studying the stars. And in c.725 the Northumbrian monk the Venerable Bede, often referred to as the father of English history, wrote *On the Reckoning of Time*. This provided the definitive solution to the long-discussed problem of establishing the date of the Easter full moon; it also described ancient calendars and views of the cosmos. The reader was supplied with practical instructions for calculating the motion of the Sun and Moon through the zodiac, too.

The Carolingian Renaissance between the eighth and ninth centuries saw a renewed enthusiasm for learning from the Roman writers, encouraged by the emperor Charlemagne. However, it wasn't until the second half of the tenth century, when Gerbert of Aurillac made his aforementioned quest to Spain for Islamic knowledge, that study of ancient knowledge began to transition to the development of the new. By the early eleventh century, scholars such as Hermann of Reichenau were writing Latin texts on how to use the astrolabe, and others such as Walcher of Malvern were exploring the instrument's use for observing the times of eclipses to question the data tables of the classical writers.

OPPOSITE: *For most of history the constellations were believed to be inextricably linked with the health of the human body, as illustrated by this c.1416 anatomical 'zodiac man'. In the picture, each sign of the zodiac is shown to correspond with a body part. Pisces is linked to the feet; Aries, with the ram's sacred associations, marks the head. The Latin inscriptions in the four corners expand on the medicinal properties of the zodiac signs. Medical astrology saw a desperate surge in popularity during the fourteenth century, with the devastation of the Black Death.*

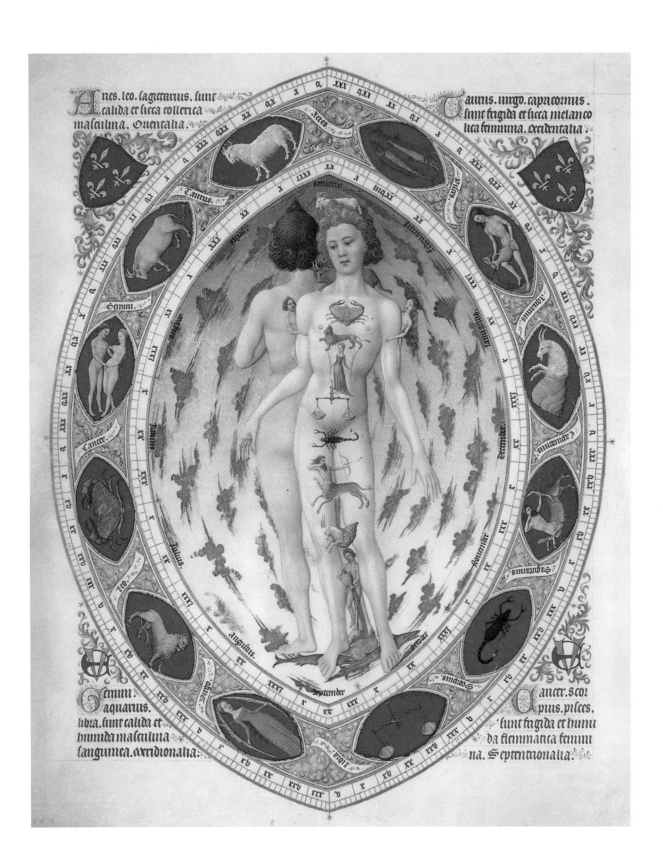

THE NEW STUDY OF THE SKY

The eleventh century saw great changes in Western Europe. Among many other developments, the explosion in urban development brought with it a change of venue for the study of the sky, from monasteries and cathedrals to new centralized arenas of learning – universities. One can forget just how long a history some European academic institutions enjoy. It is strange to think that Oxford University, for example, predates the Aztec civilization. As early as 1096, teaching had begun in the town, and by 1249 it had grown into a fully fledged university with students housed at the school's three original halls of residence of University, Balliol and Merton Colleges. The founding of the Aztec civilization, marked by the establishing of the city of Tenochtitlán by the Mexica at Lake Texcoco, did not take place until 1325.

The European centres of learning began to receive an influx of Islamic and classical source material following the conquest of Toledo by Alfonso VI of León and Castile in 1085, which marked the first time a major city in Muslim Spain was captured by Christian forces. As Islam receded from the Iberian Peninsula, translators such as Gerard of Cremona descended on the newly accessible libraries like starving men on a Jacobean feast.

OPPOSITE: *Circular rotae illustrations from a late twelfth-century English manuscript written to be a scientific textbook for monks, drawing on cosmographical knowledge of early Christian writers such as Bede and Isidore of Seville. The wheel-shaped rotae were a popular design template throughout the Middle Ages as they presented complex information simply and clearly, in the divine simplicity of a circle.*

Canis Major, otherwise known as Sirius, the 'Dog Star', the brightest point of light in the night sky, from a twelfth-century astronomical miscellany. Here Sirius is filled with poetry describing its mythological origins.

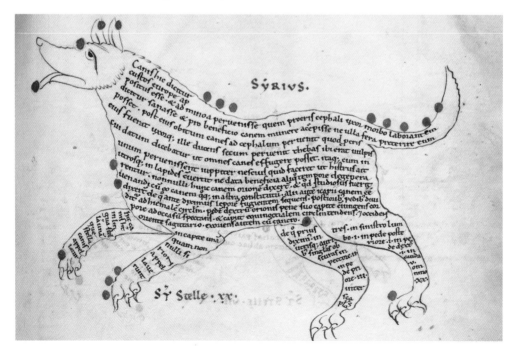

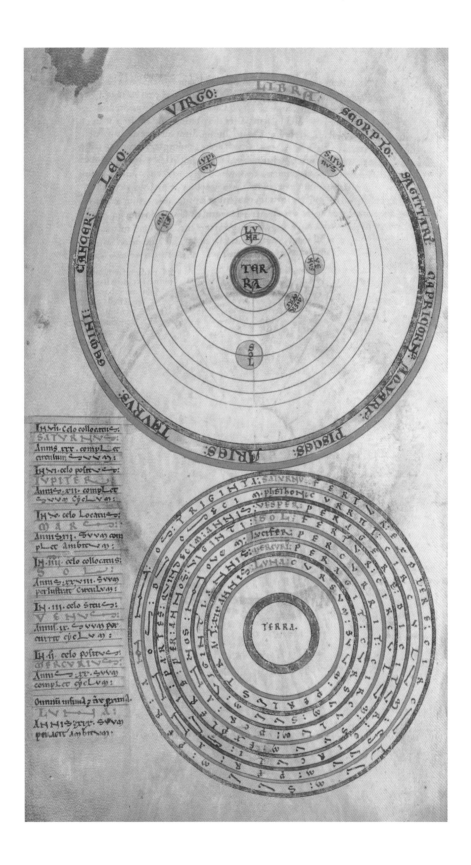

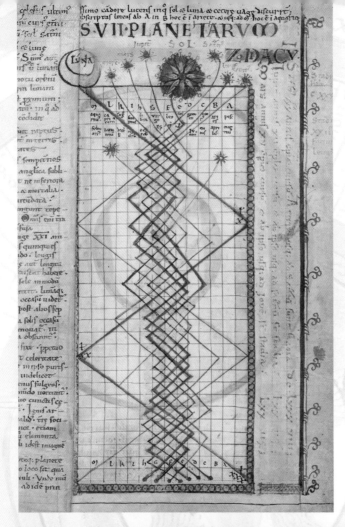

The *Liber Floridus* (*'Book of Flowers'*) is a medieval French encyclopaedia compiled by Lambert, Canon of Saint-Omer 1090–1120, from c.192 earlier works, including those of Isidore of Seville. The highly illustrated text explains everything from mythical creatures, botany, to how the world will end, as well as displaying these diagrams of twelfth-century astronomical understanding.

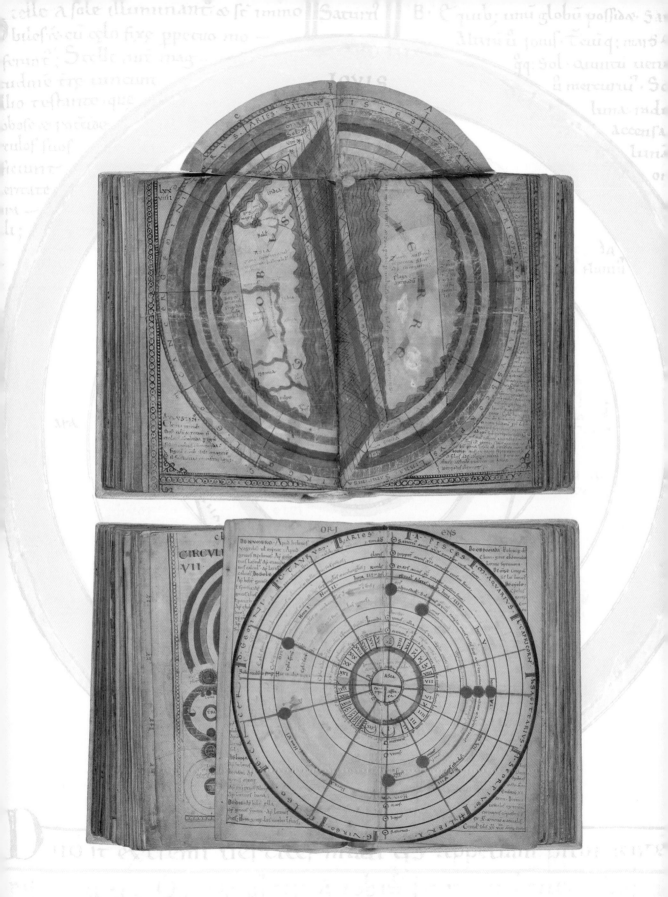

Cremona rapidly translated at least seventy-one astronomical works including the Toledan Tables of al-al-Zarqālī, which allowed the prediction of planetary positions for any time, and also produced his influential translation of Ptolemy's *Almagest* from an Arabic copy (a version in the original Greek was not found until later in the fifteenth century).

By this time it was Paris that had become the European centre of learning, and the Faculty of Arts there was most delighted with the continuing influx of these newly translated cosmological works, for with their Aristotelian (i.e. non-Christian) basis they fell within its purview, and far outside the more respected theological section.

With such enrichment from classical sources, the validity of the Arts was better defended. There was now a scientific advocacy to denude the supremacy of Church authority, especially with the advent of a new form of thought and learning known as scholasticism, which had grown from the transition of study from monastery to university. A key figure of this movement was the Italian Dominican friar, philosopher and jurist Thomas Aquinas (1225–1274), who demonstrated with his ideas of 'natural' theology that the mysteries of God and the mysteries of physics and cosmology could be investigated with the same rational approach, using biblical and classical sources.

This reconciliation of classical thought with Christian belief elevated the academic status of authorities such as Aristotle and Ptolemy, to be consulted by students who previously had little but the Bible to reach for in search of answers. This resulted, of course, in little actual scientific progress in this pre-Copernican period – answers were sought in past assertions, rather than in new observations and empirical investigations. Besides, at this stage it was the job of universities to educate, not conduct research. As their shelves began to creak under the weight of new translations, introductory summaries such as those of Paris-based Oxford scholar John of Holywood (1195–1256), known as Sacrobosco, were produced to initiate the student to the accumulation of knowledge with short, clear accounts of the Ptolemaic cosmology.

And yet, though Ptolemy's famous work *De sphaera mundi* ('On the Sphere of the World') was accompanied by diagrams of the concentric spheres, still the actual mapping of the heavens did not exist.

OPPOSITE: *Hildegard of Bingen (c.1098–1179) was a German Benedictine abbess, writer and mystic. She wrote theological, botanical and medicinal texts, but is perhaps best known for her visions, twenty-six of which formed the basis of her work* Sci vias Domini *('Know the Ways of the Lord'), in which she describes the universe as taking the shape of a 'cosmic egg'. 'By this supreme instrument in the figure of an egg, and which is the universe',* she writes, *'invisible and eternal things are manifested.'*

THE SEA ABOVE THE SKY

While celestial cartography awaited its invention, the
synthesis of the Aristotelian spheres with the Christian
picture of the universe left fundamental questions: for
example, by what force was the starry sphere, the backdrop
of the planetary theatre, caused to move in its gradual

rotation? How did this relate to the heavens created on the first day, recorded in Genesis? And what of the 'waters *above* the firmament' of the same passage, supposedly lying above the visible sky?

The last query led to a quite wonderful literal interpretation – of an overhead ocean. This mythical belief is recorded in England as late as the sixteenth century. There existed, it was thought, a great sea above the sky, navigated by flying vessels, completely invisible to those on the ground. Hunting for references to the myth takes us surprisingly far back. John Stow's *Annales, or a General Chronicle of England* (1580), which furnished Shakespeare with ideas and imagery for several of his plays, includes a report of a group of riders travelling from Bodmin to Fowey in Cornwall in May 1580, who witnessed a vast, enveloping fog appearing in the sky before them 'much like unto a sea', out of which materialized a huge castle. As they gazed upwards, a fleet of what seemed like warships sailed over their heads, closely trailed by a succession of smaller boats. The dazzling naval flyover lasted for about an hour.

Three hundred years before this, the English author Gervase of Tilbury created his *Otia Imperialia* ('Recreation for an Emperor') c.1214, for his patron, Emperor Otto IV. Also known as *The Book of Marvels*, the work is a miscellany of

Opposite: The Coeli stellati Christiani haemisphaerium posterius *map (1660) features the work of the Bavarian lawyer and amateur astronomer Julius Schiller, the first to abandon mythology and draw the constellations using Christian symbolism.*

Detail from William M. Timlin's The Ship That Sailed to Mars *(1923).*

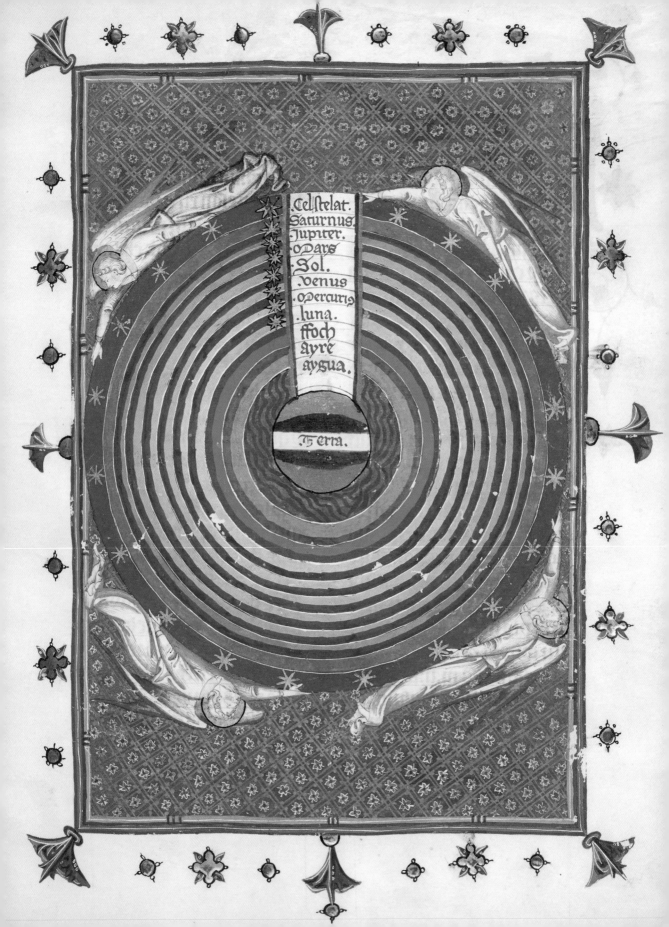

.Cel stelat.
Saturnus.
Jupiter.
Mars
Sol.
venus
Mercuri9
luna.
ffoch
ayre
aygua.

Terra.

wonders packed with myths and legends to thrill its imperial reader, including the report from England of there being a sea above the sky:

> One Sunday, the people of a village in England were coming out of church on a thick cloudy day when they saw the anchor of a ship hooked to one of the tombstones; the cable, which was tightly stretched, hanging down from the air. The people were astonished, and while they were consulting about it, suddenly they saw the rope move as though someone was trying to pull up the anchor. It was held fast by the stone, however, and a great noise was heard in the air, like the shouting of sailors. Presently a man was seen sliding down the cable for the purpose of unfixing the anchor; and when he had just loosened it, the villagers seized hold of him, but as he struggled in their hands he quickly died, just as though he had been drowned. About an hour after, the sailors above, hearing no more of their comrade, cut the cable and sailed away. In memory of this extraordinary event, the people of the village made the hinges of the church doors out of the iron of the anchor, and there they are still to be seen.

Earlier still is the writing of St Agobard, Archbishop of Lyon (AD c.779–840), who tells of a French belief in the cloud realm 'Magonia' in his work *De grandine et tonitruis* ('On Hail and Thunder'). Agobard lays out rational arguments against the various superstitious theories of 'weather magic', and writes of the contemporary belief in 'Magonia', a cloud realm sailed by villainous pirates in cahoots with Frankish weather wizards known as *tempestarii* ('storm sorcerers'). The magicians were thought to conjure up storms to batter the crops on the ground, which were then easily gathered and pilfered by the aerial sailors.

We can, in fact, find a similar idea in the official ancient Roman lists of *prodigia*. These were unusual occurrences thought to be signs of divine displeasure – any such observation was to be reported immediately as part of a Roman's civic duty. Titus Livius (64 or 59 BC–AD 17) quotes *prodigia* in his *History of Rome* 21.62 and 42.2 and mentions: 'Something that looked like ships gleamed down from the sky... Something that looked like a big fleet was said to have been seen in the sky at Lanuvium, near Rome.' This was a mirage, most likely – but also the earliest 'UFO' report on record.

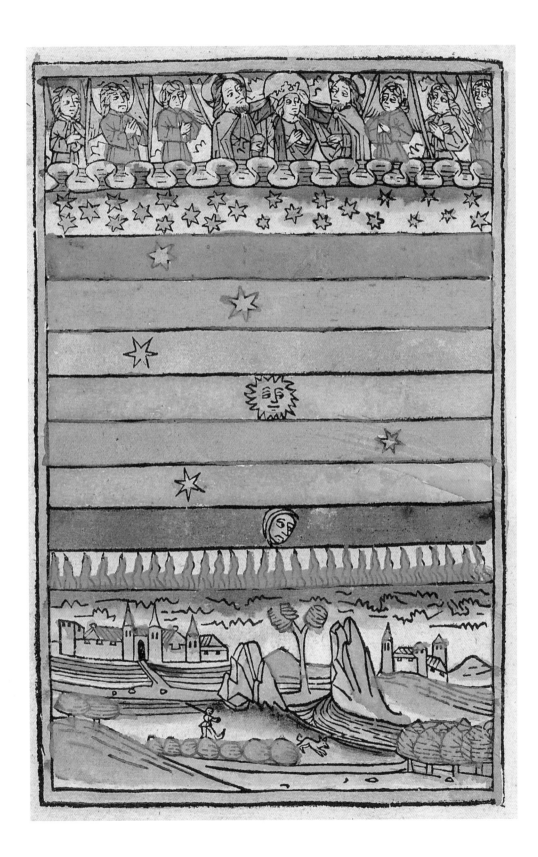

CAPTURING THE COSMOS: CLOCKWORK AND THE PRINTING PRESS

Having explained the idea of crystalline spheres of the ancient Greeks, which was held as the prevailing cosmic theory in Europe following the rediscovery of Ptolemy's works, the question remained as to the mysterious force that drove their rotation. In artworks of the fourteenth and fifteenth century, we find depictions of an offered solution derived from the writings of the sixth-century Christian mystic referred to as Pseudo-Dionysius the Areopagite, who described the hierarchy of the angels in Heaven. If God, the prime mover, imparted power to turn the outermost concentric starry ring, then perhaps it was officers of this angelic order that each

OPPOSITE: *Gustave Doré's illustration of a concentric Paradise, from Dante's* Divine Comedy.

The Creation of The World and the Expulsion from Paradise *(1445) by Giovanni di Paolo, shows God imparting an impulse to turn the outer ring of a concentric cosmos.*

controlled the movement of the remaining spheres. The
French philosopher Jean Buridan countered this idea in the
fourteenth century by adapting an earlier theory of 'impetus'
or motive force (a precursor to the modern concept of inertia),
and arguing that, as the heavens were made of quintessence,
in their perfection there could be no friction. Therefore, he
suggested, the great impulse that God had first imparted at
the Creation, like a clockmaker initiating the first swing of
the pendulum, would continue to turn the sphere in perpetuity.
'And those impetuses which He impressed in the celestial
bodies', he wrote, 'were not decreased or corrupted afterwards,
because there was no inclination of the celestial bodies for
other movements. Nor was there resistance which would
be corruptive or repressive of that impetus.'

It wasn't just with intellectual theorizing that invention
took shape in this medieval state. While astronomical
observatories would not arrive in Europe until much later,
with Tycho Brahe in the late sixteenth century, in the
fourteenth century a different type of innovation appeared:
clockwork. The sophisticated technology used by the Greeks
in the first century BC to create the Antikythera mechanism
(see The Ancient Greeks entry on page 51) had long since been
lost, but amid the flood of Islamic knowledge pouring into
Europe towards the end of the first millennium the science
of clockwork mechanisms once again began to develop.

*Dante guides the reader to his
sources by including many as
characters. In the fourth sphere
of the Sun ('The Wise'), for
example, Dante and Beatrice
encounter twelve wise men that
include Dionysius, Bede, Albertus
Magnus and Thomas Aquinas.*

Monasteries had for centuries used primitive forms of water clocks to help indicate the correct time of prayer, but before his death in 1336 Richard of Wallingford, Abbot of St Albans, had completed the construction of a mechanical astronomical clock that was a marvel of its age. Not only did it tell the time in hours and minutes, but using differential gears the device acted as a moving model of the universe. A rotating Moon showed the lunar phases and eclipses (the average motion of which was within 1.8 parts per million of the true value), and possibly also planetary motion – the uncertainty is due to the fact, although most of Richard's original designs survived, the clock itself

Illustration from The Book of Knowledge of Ingenious Mechanical Devices *(1206), a treatise on fantastic devices invented by the Persian author Al-Jazari. His elephant clock was especially intricate: every half hour, the bird on the dome whistled; the man below dropped a ball into the dragon's mouth; and the driver hit the elephant with his goad.*

was destroyed during Henry VIII's reformation and the dissolution of St Albans Abbey in 1539.

The astrarium of Giovanni de' Dondi (1318–1389), an astronomer and engineer in Padua, was completed in 1364 and met with even greater fame. Using a complex mechanism of 107 wheels and pinions, it modelled the planetary system with mathematical precision. Together with the clock movement was an annual calendar wheel of the liturgical moveable feasts, planetary dials and a twenty-four-hour *Primum Mobile* dial that reproduced the diurnal motion of the stars and the annual motion of the Sun against the background of stars. Though the astrarium was also destroyed, likely in the sacking of Mantua in 1630, de' Dondi left detailed descriptions which have allowed reconstructions to be made. Pieced together entirely by hand, it was a work 'full of artifice… and carved with a skill never attained by the expert hand of any craftsman', wrote an admiring Giovanni Manzini of Pavia in 1388. 'I conclude that there was never invented an artifice so excellent and marvellous and of such genius.'

The clock face as we would recognize it today appeared later in the fifteenth century, and when one compares it with the face of an astrolabe the direct influence in design is unmistakable. In the face of a clock the cosmos is captured in its circular form, its chaos brought under mechanical control, the hands modelled on the bar of the astrolabe turning within the same 360 degrees as the spheres of the heavens. It is a remarkable thing to consider that today, in the form of the mechanical watch, we wear on our wrists the medieval universe.

As well as the astronomical clock, the same inventive ingenuity was applied to navigation. Ships were venturing farther than ever before, leaving the coastlines behind as Europe sailed into the Age of Exploration, traditionally dated loosely from the beginning of the fifteenth century to the end of the eighteenth century. For guidance to the right parallel, the measurement of latitude was therefore crucial (the problem of longitude would not be solved until the 1760s with John Harrison's marine chronometer). During daylight hours, the mariner's astrolabe was used to take a measurement of the Sun's altitude at noon, which the navigator would cross-reference with tables that listed every position of the Sun above and

ABOVE: *A mid-twentieth century reconstruction of de Dondi's famous astrarium, a mechanical realization of the Ptolemaic universe.*

below the celestial equator throughout the year. Measuring one's latitude at night was slightly trickier. An instrument known as a 'nocturnal', or sometimes 'nocturlabe', was created by adapting the astrolabe to be based not on solar but sidereal, or star, time. Using this clever device, the navigator could not only tell the time at night, but also judge his latitude by measuring the altitude of the Pole Star and working out its position relative to the celestial Pole. Often mariners' nocturnals were cut with notches along the edges so that the operator could perform the reading in pitch darkness.

The invention that had a seismic effect on astronomical learning, and indeed the communication of information as a whole, came c.1440 when the German goldsmith Johannes Gutenberg introduced the moveable-type printing press in Europe.* Printed copies of manuscripts transformed scientific study. No longer was it necessary for scribes to painstakingly reproduce by hand the great reference works. However beautiful the calligraphy, each manuscript carried with it the caveat that errors made by previous copies might be also reproduced. With the complicated formulas and figures involved in astronomy, inevitably new mistakes were also introduced.

The clearest windows into gauging the understanding of an age are the contemporary texts designed to teach. With the arrival of the printing press, we gain our clearest picture yet, as a new industry of text production was kick-started. One of the most famous names in this area is that of Johannes Müller von Königsberg of Vienna, known as Regiomontanus. At the behest of the papal legate and humanist scholar Basilios Bessarion, Regiomontanus and his friend Georg von Peuerbach produced an accurate, abridged translation of Ptolemy's *Almagest* from the original Greek into Latin. Von Peuerbach fell unwell in the process, and made Regiomontanus promise to finish the work in the event of his death. *Epytoma in Almagestum* ('The Epitome of the Almagest'), which was half the length of Ptolemy's original work but considerably greater in clarity, was printed in 1496 and was instrumental in disseminating the Alexandrian's ideas throughout Europe.

As well as water clocks and mechanical and candle clocks, a timekeeping device known as a fragrance clock appeared in China in the Song dynasty (960–1279). These featured sticks of incense with specific burning rates, dropping weights with a clatter onto dishes at regular intervals.

Opposite: A c.1570 German 'mirror clock', with various celestial measurements. An example of a bridge between divine order and Renaissance science, these devices were also known as 'monstrance clocks' for their similarity to the Catholic receptacle for the consecrated host.

*But not, as is popularly believed in the West, the world. In Asia, moveable-type printing had been taking place long before. From AD c.1040, for example, the Chinese inventor Bi Sheng was printing with characters carved out of clay and set in an iron plate.

To accompany his astrological work Archidoxa *(1569), Leonhard Thurneysser published the* Astrolabium *in 1575, with numerous volvelles (wheeled paper instruments).*

In fact, the work of Regiomontanus would have affect even farther afield – it was his almanac of 1474, which contained astronomical tables predicting dates of celestial events, that Christopher Columbus took with him on his fourth voyage to the New World. Stranded on the island now known as Jamaica and desperate for food, Columbus informed the local Arawak natives that the Spaniard's god was displeased with their lack of assistance, and would show his displeasure by rendering the Moon 'inflamed with wrath'. Sure enough, on 29 February 1504 the Moon transformed into a dull red sphere. According to Columbus's son, Ferdinand, the Arawaks were terrified by the predicted sight of the bloody Moon, and 'with great howling and lamentation came running from every direction to the ships laden with provisions and beseeching the admiral to intercede with his god on their behalf'. Columbus, of course, had used Regiomontanus's almanac to calculate the appearance of a lunar eclipse.

Regiomontanus continued his printing output until his death in 1476. His observations were drawn on by Tycho Brahe (see Tycho Brahe entry on page 124), Johannes Kepler (see Johannes Kepler entry on page 130) and others; but, most significantly, they were instrumental in shaping the ideas of a young Polish astronomer named Nicolaus Copernicus, who would soon trigger an intellectual revolution.

More than a thousand years after it was written, Ptolemy's work was still being translated and discussed. In the frontispiece to Regiomontanus's Epytoma in Almagestum, *the Renaissance author and the long-dead Alexandrian sit together beneath an armillary sphere.*

CELESTIAL PHENOMENA: PART ONE

ABOVE AND LEFT: *A panel of illustrations from the* Kometenbuch *('Comet Book'), an album of miniature watercolour sketches of comets and meteors recorded from the previous centuries. Produced in Flanders or northeast France in 1587, nothing is known of the author and illustrator.*

LEFT: *From the c.1550* Augsburger wunderzeichenbuch *('Augsburger Book of Wonders'), the caption reads: 'In AD 1007, a wondrous comet appeared. It gave off fire and flames in every direction. It was seen in Germany and Welschland and it fell on to the Earth.'*

RIGHT: *Another from the* Augsburger wunderzeichenbuch: *'In the year AD 1401, a large comet with a peacock tail appeared in the sky over Germany. This was followed by a most severe plague in Swabia.'*

Strange celestial phenomena filled the skies over Nuremberg on 14 April 1561. The citizens described a large, black, triangular object and hundreds of spheres, cylinders and other strange objects flying around the sky. Often pointed to as the first illustrated 'UFO' sighting, it's thought that, if it did occur, the event might have been an atmospheric optical phenomenon called a 'sun dog'.

(See also Celestial Phenomena: Part Two on page 208.)

MESOAMERICA

The dazzling southern skies played a significant role in the cultures of the pre-Hispanic peoples of Mesoamerica. For the Incas, who ruled from modern Ecuador to Chile, the Mayu (Milky Way) was a heavenly life-giving river, matching its terrestrial twin, the Urubamba River in the Sacred Valley, high in the Andes Mountains in what is now Peru. Though the Incas saw patterns in the constellations, it was in the negative space of the darkness between stars in the Mayu that they found their celestial creatures – 'dark cloud' constellations that were viewed as animals drinking at the sky-river's edge.

The Aztec calendar stone, thought to have been carved c.1502–1521, showing the calendar system used by the Aztecs and other pre-Columbian peoples of central Mexico.

Venus as the morning star, from a nineteenth-century facsimile of the Codex Borgia, *a pre-Hispanic divinatory manuscript.*

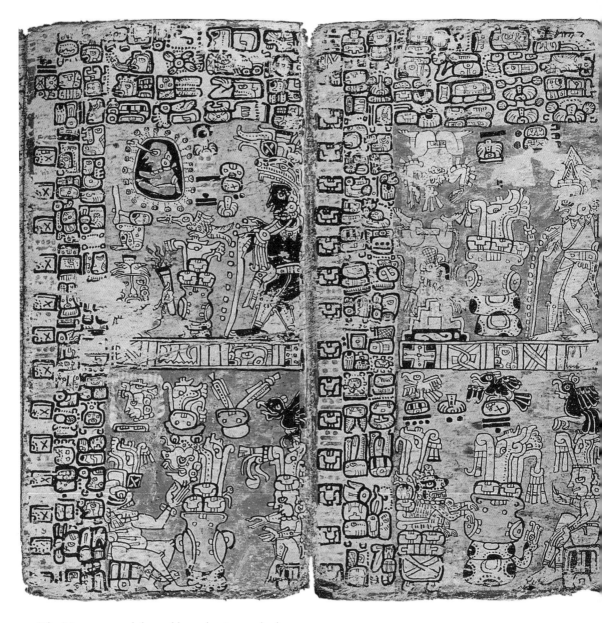

The Maya, meanwhile, and later the Aztecs, had sophisticated mathematical techniques for timekeeping and calculations for advanced calendars, though nothing in the way of star maps has survived from the Central American cultures. Their astronomy was tied to their extensive belief tree of gods and demons, while the sacred Sun formed the basis of their 365-day agricultural calendar cycle called *xiuhpōhualli* ('year count'). This was combined with a 260-day ritual cycle called *tōnalpōhualli* ('day count'), which rolled together in a fifty-two-year 'century', otherwise known as the 'calendar round'.

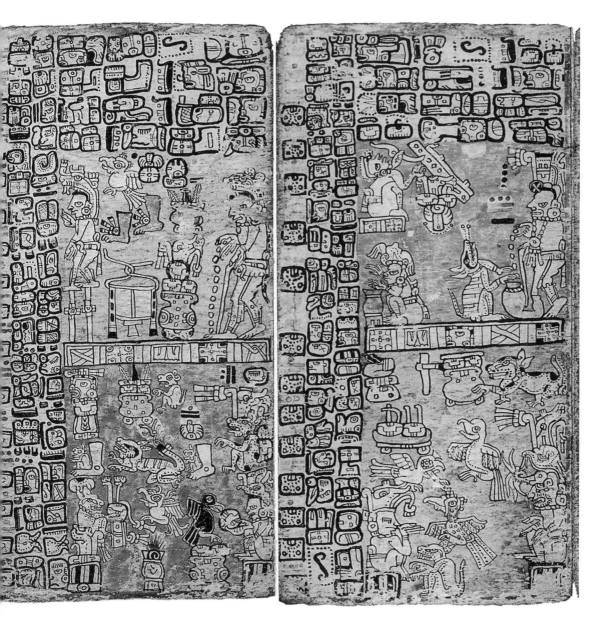

The longest of their calculations was the dating of the creation of the universe back to 3114 BC – why this exact year was chosen is unknown. The Sun was believed to have come into existence as the result of a god sacrificing himself for mankind, and was thought to be the fifth one to have existed, the previous four Suns having been destroyed with previous earthly disasters. Venus was also of particular importance: the feathered serpent deity Quetzalcoatl was believed to take the form of the morning star, which was important as sighting the planet heralded the coming rain season.

A section of the Madrid Codex, *one of three surviving pre-Columbian Mayan texts from AD c.900 to 1521. The seated figure featured in the top left section is believed to be a Mayan astronomer.*

THE SCIE

In the fourteenth century, the intellectual fabric of Europe began to transform with the cultural movement known as the Renaissance. Underpinned by the humanistic rediscovery of classical Greek philosophy and knowledge, and a nostalgia for a perceived scholarly golden era of antiquity, Europe revelled in a rediscovery of artistic, architectural, political, scientific and literary traditions. Timed perfectly with the invention of printing in the West, these waves of influence rolled rapidly out of Italy and rippled through the entire continent.

NTIFIC SKY

'And yet it moves.'

Attributed to Galileo Galilei, in response to being forced by the Catholic Church to recant the idea that Earth orbits the Sun.

In the field of astronomy this sea change would occur much later, towards the end of the fifteenth century. Ptolemy's second-century geocentric (Earth-centred) concept of the universe continued to be the largely accepted model, despite suggestions of a heliocentric (Sun-centred) structure having been made at least as early as the fourth century BC by Aristarchus of Samos (310–230 BC). (The notion had been ruled impossible by Aristotelian physics and dismissed.) The Ptolemaic universe dominated, but the voices questioning its accuracy grew louder. Notable among this critical chorus were the teachers of Poland's University of Kraków. At that time, the institution had two highly renowned departments dedicated to the advancement of astronomic sciences: mathematics and astronomy founded in 1405; and the department of astrology, referred to as 'practical astronomy' due to its ties with medical science, in 1453. The Kraków school of astronomy was arguably the most distinguished in Europe. The faculty had made known their objections to Ptolemy's equant – the mathematical concept he introduced in the *Almagest* to account for the observed motion of planets – on the grounds that it clashed with the principle of uniform circular motion (the motion of an object travelling at a constant speed on a circular path). The comprehensive education the school offered was precisely why it was sought out in 1491 by an 18-year-old student named Nicolaus Copernicus.

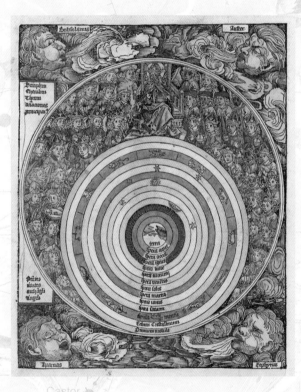

A hybrid of Christian and Aristotelian belief, showing a universe composed of concentric spheres, framed by an enthroned God flanked by his hierarchy of angels. From the Nuremberg Chronicle, *1493.*

OPPOSITE: *The Caprarola fresco of constellations, painted inside the Palazzo Farnese, Rome, by an anonymous artist in 1575.*

THE COPERNICAN REVOLUTION

The rejection of the Ptolemaic model by Nicolaus Copernicus (1473–1543) is traditionally dated to the publishing of his *De revolutionibus orbium coelestium* ('On the Revolutions of the Heavenly Spheres') in 1543, printed on the day of his death (though an earlier manuscript suggests the idea was resident in his mind from at least 1510). It would initiate a complete re-envisioning of the understood picture of the universe. What led him to form such a subversive idea? The problematic equant (described as 'a relation that nature abhors' by the sixteenth-century astronomer and Copernican acolyte Georg Joachim Rheticus) was one point of dispute. Another was the Moon in the Ptolemaic model. Approached mathematically, it simply didn't make sense. In Ptolemaic astronomy, the planets and Moon travel in epicycles (small circles), which in turn travel on larger circles around Earth called deferents. In Ptolemy's *Almagest*, the Moon's epicycle is bizarrely large in relation to its deferent, which results in the Moon's height above Earth varying wildly. From simple observation, this was clearly not accurate. Applying modern mathematics to Ptolemy's surviving works showed his system was erratic. The planets were explained separately, but not as a whole. It certainly did not fit with the Platonic view of Nature's cosmos as an elegant, harmonious system. Copernicus was fascinated by his predecessors' lack of success in rationalizing the system as a fully working symphony: 'They are just like someone taking from different places hands, feet, head, and the other limbs', he wrote, 'no doubt depicted very well but not modelled from the same body and not matching one another – so that such parts would produce a monster rather than a man.' After thirty years of data gathering between 1510 and 1540, Copernicus had refined his idea. His model of the cosmos placed the Sun at the centre, with Earth now a planet, the Moon its satellite, and the six planets arranged in order. He permitted Rheticus to publish a first report of his work and, meeting no fierce reaction, allowed *De revolutionibus...* to be printed in Nuremberg in 1543.

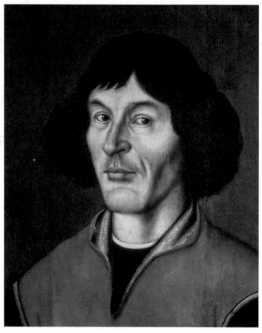

Nicolaus Copernicus.

In the centre of all resides the Sun [goes the famous passage of the book], for in this most beautiful temple who would place this lamp in another or better place than that from which it can illuminate the whole at one and the same time? As a matter of fact, not inappropriately do some call it the lantern of the universe; others, its mind; and others still, its ruler… And thus, the Sun, as if seated on a kingly throne, governs the family of planets that wheel around it.

Shifting perspective to Earth being a planetary satellite of the Sun, the Copernican model suddenly offered simple answers to long unsolved cosmic riddles. The puzzle of the retrograde

The Copernican theory of a heliocentric universe, illustrated by Andreas Cellarius, 1660.

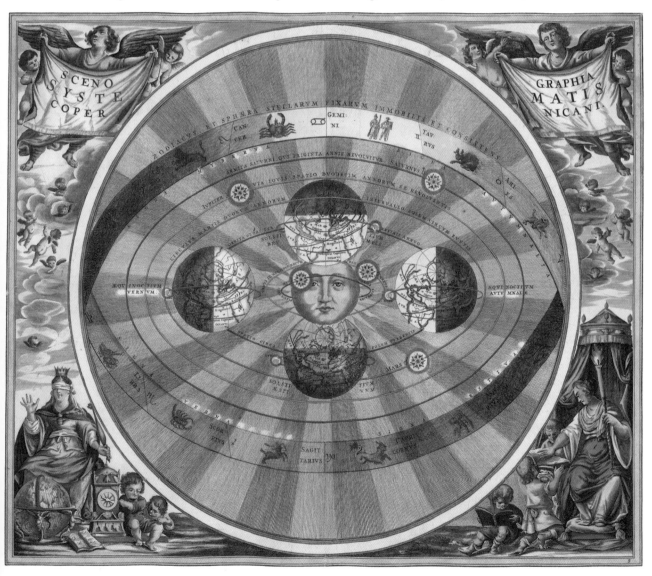

motions, for example, when the planets temporarily appear to us to be moving backwards. With the Copernican solution, this now made sense: as we move around the Sun, inside of, say, Mars's solar orbit, for most of the time we appear to be moving in the same direction as that planet. But for the short time at the point where we pass by Mars on our shorter solar orbit, the planet *appears* to us to head backwards. Here was the graceful model of simplicity that had been sought for so long.

The new system also, of course, raised new questions – most profoundly on the size of the cosmos. If Earth orbited the Sun (at a distance Copernicus erroneously calculated as c.4.5 million miles/7 million km), then there should be a parallax effect experienced when observing the stars – that is, they should appear to move, as our vantage point from the moving Earth is always changing. This effect was clearly absent, suggesting the universe was of a much greater size than conceived, the stars so far away and apart that the distance of Earth's journey around the Sun paled in comparison. Copernicus was also calling into question one of the fundamental pillars of Aristotelian physics. This was the rule that celestial bodies, elements of earth and water, and any tossed objects, fall towards their natural place – the centre of the universe. So if Earth had never been that centre, then (to great consternation) contemporary physical theories of weight and motion were no longer sufficient. Everything would have to be rethought. How was it that Earth was spherical, for example, and what made it turn? And how could it be racing around the Sun, when we on its surface have no sensation of this dizzying velocity?

A celebrated cosmic diagram that accompanied Thomas Digges's A Perfit Description of the Caelestial Orbes (1576). *The English mathematician was the first in Britain to champion the Copernican system, and went farther, discarding the idea of a shell of fixed stars in favour of there being an endless amount of stars in an infinite universe. In England, this diagram helped the idea become part of the Copernican theory.*

The Astronomicum caesareum (1540), considered the greatest sixteenth-century masterpiece of the printing art. An astrolabe in book form, it was designed by Petrus Apianus for his patrons, the Hapsburg rulers

Emperor Charles V and his brother Ferdinand, to allow the calculation of planetary alignments, lunar eclipses and stellar positioning, using the ingenious paper instruments with moveable wheel parts known as volvelles or Apian wheels.

TYCHO BRAHE

With *De revolutionibus…* raising these questions but offering few answers, the scientific revolution got underway as it fell to others to resolve or rebut the 'radical' Copernican structure with natural laws, and transform astronomy from a science of geometry to one of physics. The printed map had arrived in the late fifteenth century, and with it the revival of Ptolemy's system of applying geographical coordinates for more realistic representation (part of a Renaissance obsession with measurement). The first printed celestial map soon followed in 1515 (see image opposite), produced by the German master artist Albrecht Dürer (1471–1528) in the style of the earliest known manuscript European star map – the Vienna manuscript (see image above).

In the Vienna manuscript, the earliest known European celestial map of the northern skies, the stars were identified with numbers referencing Ptolemy's star catalogue. This was the style that all celestial maps would follow. From the anonymous work De Composicione Sphere Solide, *1440.*

Astronomy now transformed into a science that prioritized empirical observation over classical authority. Only through studying the sky with sharper accuracy, using developed instruments and improved techniques, could the clues to the cosmos be uncovered. Instrumental in this change of approach was Tycho Brahe (1546–1601), the golden-nosed* Danish noble who had explored a passion for astronomy with assiduous observation since the age of sixteen, when he had witnessed Jupiter overtaking Saturn in the night sky for the first time in twenty years, and found that both the Ptolemaic-based Alfonsine Tables, first compiled in 1483, and post-Copernican data sets failed to accurately predict the event.

Then came an explosion in the sky. In 1572 Brahe spotted what appeared to be a new star in the constellation Cassiopeia, an astonishing phenomenon that – on the traditional understanding of Aristotle's law of a perfect, unchanging cosmos – was considered impossible. The blazing light Brahe sighted was a supernova, a star exploding at the end of its life

Tycho Brahe.

The first European printed star chart of the northern sky by the great artist Albrecht Dürer, published 1515 in Nuremberg, Germany.

*Brahe lost the bridge of his nose in a sword duel in the pitch dark with a fellow Dane, Manderup Parsberg, over a disagreement about a mathematical formula, on 29 December 1566. For the rest of his life, he wore a prosthetic glued in place, famously made of gold, although in a testament to the power of human curiosity in 2010 his body was exhumed, and through chemical analysis it was revealed that the prosthetic had, in fact, been made of brass. (He may, it was conceded, have also worn a gold nose for special occasions.)

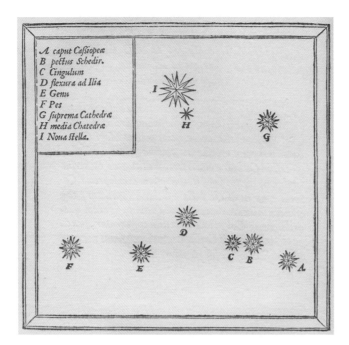

A caput Cassiopeæ
B pectus Schedir.
C Cingulum
D flexura ad Ilia
E Genu
F Pes
G suprema Cathedræ
H media Chatedræ
I Noua stella.

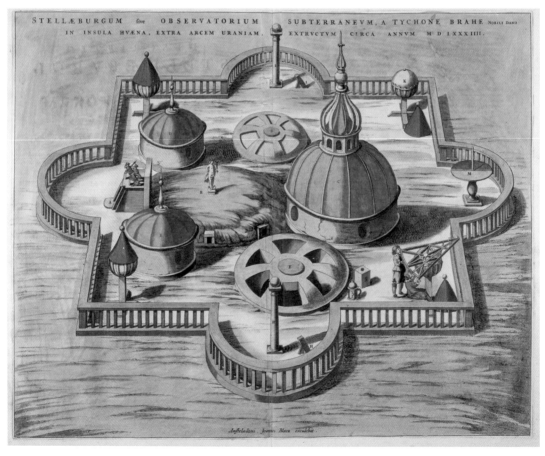

STELLÆBURGUM sive OBSERVATORIUM SUBTERRANEVM, A TYCHONE BRAHE NOBILI DANO
IN INSULA HVÆNA, EXTRA ARCEM URANIAM, EXTRVCTVM CIRCA ANNVM M D LXXXIIII.

Amstelædami, Joannes Blaeu excudebat.

– in this case, one that is now referred to as SN 1572 or Tycho's Supernova. Clearly the heavens were, in fact, an arena of change. The appearance of a dazzling comet splitting the sky in 1577 contributed further to this realization. The temporary appearance and striking velocity of comets had, until that point, led to their classification as being not celestial but terrestrial, thought to be an atmospheric phenomenon and so belonging to the study of meteorology. Having witnessed the comet of 1577, Brahe was able to show that this was a phenomenon that took place much farther away than previously thought, that travelled among the planets and was very much a part of the celestial realm. This raised an obvious question – if the cosmos consisted of solid transparent spheres, carrying the planets with their turning motion, then how could a comet pass through them? The answer, Brahe realized, was a simple but profound one – the spheres did not exist.

The armillary at Stjerneborg.

With the endorsement of King Frederick II of Denmark, Brahe built the first observatory in Christian Europe on the island of Ven and named it Uraniborg ('Heavenly Castle'). When that proved too small for his purposes, he built a second nearby, Stjerneborg ('Castle of the Stars'), recording observations with an army of assistants who lived on site and were equipped with new instruments such as the sextant Brahe invented to measure the angle between two stars. The result of all this industry was a meticulous catalogue of 777 stars of the northern sky. The position of each one measured multiple times to ensure accuracy, to form a collection to replace the outdated Ptolemaic tables still in use by contemporaries. (Brahe would also engrave each one into a giant celestial globe, though sadly this wondrous object has not survived.)

Inevitably, years of careful star-mapping led Brahe to form his own cosmological model – the Tychonic system. Brahe saw the simple logic of the Copernican idea, but as a committed Protestant could not reconcile it with the writings of the Old Testament that spoke of the terrestrial world at the centre of Creation. The idea that Earth was moving at speed was problematic with the ancient example of proof that it was stationary – fire an arrow into the sky, and it would fall at your feet. How could this be if the world was on the move? His solution was to argue for much of the

'Scenography of the world's construction according to Brahe', from Andreas Cellarius's celestial atlas Harmonia macrocosmica, *1660, the finest celestial atlas ever produced. The chart illustrates the Tychonic system, with the Sun, Moon and stars (shown as a ribbon with the zodiac) revolving around Earth while the other five planets revolve around the Sun.*

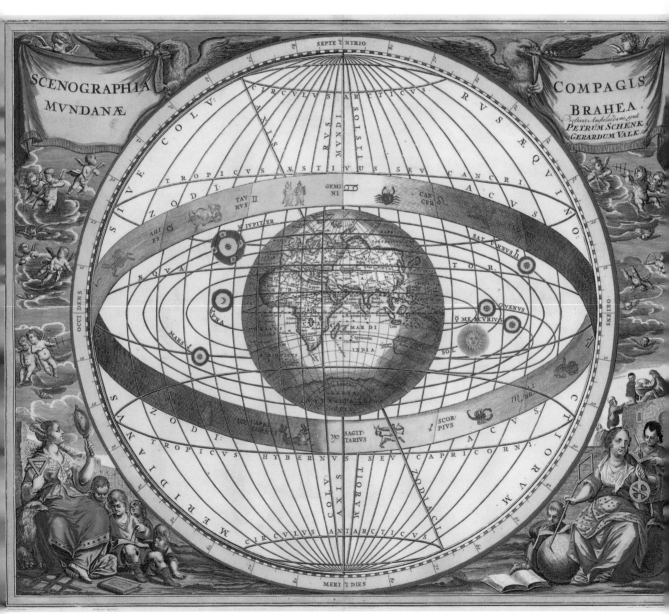

motions suggested by Copernicus, but with one major difference – it was Earth fixed in place at the centre, orbited by the Sun and Moon, while Saturn, Mars, Jupiter, Venus and Mercury were all solar satellites. Brahe also compressed the Copernican cosmos to a more credible size. Just beyond the orbit of the farthest planet lay a thin layer of space where the stars were held. Estimating the radius of this universe to be only around 14,000 Earth-radii, Brahe's cosmos was significantly smaller than the Copernican and even the Ptolemaic, which had been set at 20,000 Earth-radii.

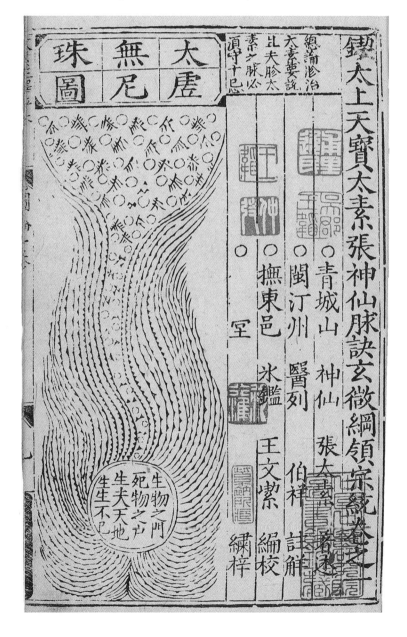

Chinese cosmology at the time of Brahe. This woodcut, dating from 1599, shows the generation of the wanwu *('myriad things') of the universe from nothingness. Through the infinite process of creation and change of Yin and Yang, the cosmos and its contents are formed.*

JOHANNES KEPLER

By the seventeenth century, the science of astronomy and mankind's image of the universe was in a disorienting phase of transition, triggered by Copernicus's reimagined geometry. Indeed, ever since the concept of celestial spheres had first been introduced in ancient Greece, it was the geometry of the cosmos that dominated the intellectual industry of the astronomer, whose job, simply put, was to develop a system to predict the movements of the planets. The question of what force drove this movement had always come second to this prime objective, mainly because the answer was simple – God (as we have seen with the idea of the impetus imparted to the turning celestial spheres by the prime mover and his angelic hierarchy). As indicated by the title of his masterwork ('On the Revolutions of the Heavenly Spheres'), even Copernicus was unwilling to abandon the basic concept of celestial spheres accounting for the planets' movement, though he made few references to the idea in the text. Brahe's demonstration of the

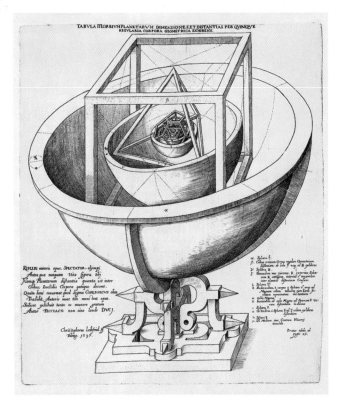

Kepler's sophisticated (and to modern minds, quite mad) model of the universe stated that each planetary sphere was divided by a different classical geometric solid. So in this diagram, for example, we can see Saturn's outermost sphere is divided from the sphere of Jupiter by a giant cube framework.

changing nature of the heavens, and the unobstructed path of comets through where these spheres should be, was a leap forward, though his preference for the geocentric model was a step back.

The German mathematician Johannes Kepler (1571–1630), a mind of remarkable genius, would introduce the study of planetary dynamics, but in tackling the question of the planets' movement he developed his own ideas on their arrangement. Having initially trained as a Lutheran minister, the simplicity of holy perfection was as much a factor in his search for

The Platonic solids, the five polyhedrals said by Aristotle to be the shapes in which the five elements – fire, earth, water, air and the incorruptible ether – took form. From Kepler's Harmonices mundi *(1619).*

answers as his admiration of the Copernican hypothesis. His faith fed his curiosity. Why would God have created the specific number of six planets? Why did they vary in distance from the Sun? His solution, which he published in *Mysterium cosmographicum* ('The Cosmographic Mystery') in 1596, was dazzling. Perhaps there was a three-dimensional geometric basis to the universe founded on the 'Platonic Solids'. These were five solid polyhedral shapes theorized by Plato in the *Timaeus* to be the compositional shape of the five classical elements: tetrahedron (four faces); cube (six); octahedron (eight); dodecahedron (twelve); and icosahedron (twenty). Kepler proposed that each of these giant solid shapes was nested in a specific order between each sphere – for five shapes to fit perfectly between six spheres – which dictated the amount of distance between them. (Astonishingly, the ratios do indeed conform to some degree.) This explanation for the varied distances between the spheres accounted for the variety in distance of the planetary paths.

At this point it's probably most helpful to consult the illustration of this idea that Kepler included in *Mysterium cosmographicum* (reproduced on page 131), to understand just how magnificently strange, yet undeniably ingenious, the concept is.

Tycho Brahe recognized the genius in Kepler's mathematical wizardry and invited him to assist in his investigation of the planets at a new observatory in Prague in 1600. Immediately Kepler set to work on the puzzle of Mars, the orbit of which was the most stubbornly peculiar to the circular model. When Brahe died a year later, Kepler took over his position and was able to enjoy privileged access to Brahe's lifelong collection of observation data. Kepler believed that the Sun rotated and exerted a mysterious force on the planets, similar to that of a magnet, and it was this force that drove the planetary orbits. But the belief in the circular path of these orbits still did not fit. Originally he had discounted an elliptical orbit as an option – surely, he reasoned, if this simple idea worked better than the circle then it would have been proven by predecessors. Using Brahe's detailed observations allowed Kepler to find that a circular orbit for Mars was inaccurate by a full eight minutes of arc (a massive discrepancy that proved the model erroneous); he also found the ellipse model instead fitted perfectly. And so was born the first of his groundbreaking

The frontispiece of Kepler's Rudolphine Tables (featuring the author in the company of Ptolemy and Copernicus), which allowed readers to find the planets in relation to the stars.

three laws of planetary motion: all planets move about the Sun in elliptical orbits, having the Sun at one focus.

Kepler's second law, which he, in fact, discovered before the first, describes the velocity of a planet moving in an elliptical orbit around the Sun. Essentially it states that a line between the Sun and a planet sweeps equal areas in equal times. So the velocity of a planet increases as it approaches the Sun, and decreases as it moves away. This second law allowed Kepler to divide up the orbit into an arbitrary number of parts, calculate the planet's position for each one, and then refer to a table, but he could not pinpoint the position of the planet at each moment because of a problem still unsolved: the speed of planets was always changing. Both laws were published in *Astronomia nova…* ('New Astronomy…') in 1609, a towering work.

With *Harmonices mundi* ('The Harmony of the World') in 1619*, Kepler revealed his third planetary motion law – that the square of the orbital period of a planet is proportional to the cube of the semi-major axis of its orbit (i.e. the direct relationship between the distance of planets from the Sun, and the length of their orbital periods).

In 1627, Kepler produced the ultimate testament to an astronomer's faith in his own innovation, an updated set of planetary tables in memory of Holy Roman Emperor Rudolf II that would be an aid in predicting the paths of celestial bodies with greater accuracy than ever before. The Rudolphine Tables, as they were known, marked the positions of 1005 stars and passed their first great test a year after Kepler's death in 1630, when the French astronomer Pierre Gassendi became the first person in history to observe Mercury pass in front of the Sun, just as Kepler had predicted.

'I measured the skies', reads Kepler's epitaph, 'now the shadows I measure. Skybound was the mind, Earthbound the body rests.' Though many fundamental questions remained – not least as to what force it was that the Sun exerted on the planets – Kepler's work effected a profound transformation with its new science of celestial dynamics. Astronomy had been transported from the realm of geometry to the field of physics.

---

*This output is all the more remarkable when one considers that, between 1615 and 1621, Kepler was simultaneously battling an accusation made against his mother Katharina of witchcraft. With the help of friends, Kepler himself defended her against the witch-hunters at her trial, and took her to Linz to be safe. However, she was arrested in 1620 and imprisoned for fourteen months, during which time she was frequently threatened with torture, but refused to confess. She was released in 1621, and died just six months later.

ABOVE: *While Kepler and Brahe performed their observations, Johann Bayer was compiling his* Uranometria (1603), *the first star atlas to map the celestial sphere. Bayer began naming stars by their constellation and with Greek letters in their perceived order of brightness: e.g. Alpha Centauri. Here, the constellation Andromeda.*

LEFT: *Virgo, the second largest constellation in the sky.*

OPPOSITE TOP: *Bayer's constellation Aquila (Eagle).*

OPPOSITE BOTTOM: *The great dragon of the Draco constellation, one of the forty-eight constellations listed by Ptolemy.*

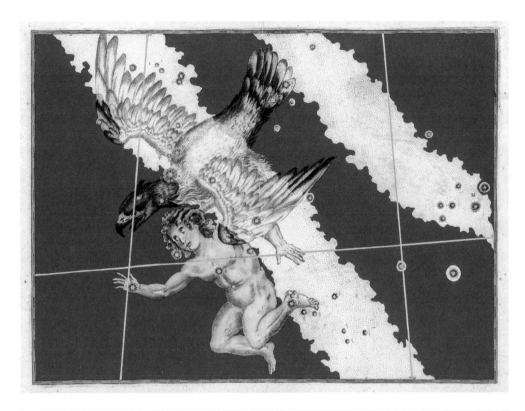

GALILEO GALILEI

Ideas as to what form the cosmos took, and supporting mythologies, varied wildly throughout the centuries and across cultures, but no matter how far the imagination roamed even the most brilliant minds of the past were restricted by the limits of the human eye. By the seventeenth century, thousands of years of naked-eye observations had picked clean the celestial realm within the extent of our gaze. This all changed in 1608 when a German–Dutch spectacle-maker called Hans Lippershey filed a patent for a device 'for seeing things far away as if they were nearby' – the earliest known telescope. The news of the 'Dutch perspective glass' (the word telescope was coined three years later by Giovanni Demisiani) with a convex lens and a concave eyepiece was carried across Europe in a Dutch diplomatic report on an ambassadorial visit from the Kingdom of Siam. The invention was seized on by members of the scientific community; from the Englishman Thomas Harriot, who by 1609 was using a six-powered form of the device, to the Italian polymath Galileo Galilei (1564–1642).

Galileo had spent the previous eighteen years teaching mathematics in Padua, but when he built and demonstrated his own eight-powered telescope, an improved version of Lippershey's design, in Venice in 1609, it was met with such amazement that he was offered the prestigious post of mathematician and philosopher to Cosimo II de' Medici, Grand Duke of Tuscany. He soon constructed in Florence a twenty-powered telescope, and with it began to make his infamous discoveries, as an ocean of new stars and celestial phenomena became visible to the human eye for the first time in history. Before placing his eye to the lens, Galileo had seen insufficient evidence for the Copernican model. Kepler had sent him a copy of *Mysterium cosmographicum* in 1597 but it had failed to convince, and indeed Copernican proponents were still rare at this time. But the discoveries Galileo made through his interrogations via the telescope's sights almost immediately overrode this scepticism.

In March 1610 Galileo published *Sidereus nuncius* ('The Starry Message'), a hasty collection of the first of his profoundly impactful discoveries, accompanied by more than seventy

OPPOSITE: *Galileo's draft of a letter he would send to Leonardo Donato, Doge of Venice, in August 1609, announcing the telescope he had built and its potential use in warfare. In the lower half of this remarkable document are his observations of the moons around Jupiter.*

Ser.mo Prin̄cipe.

Galileo Galilij Humiliss.o Seruo della Ser.a V.a inuigilan=
do assiduam.te, et cō ogni spirito p̄ potere nō solam.te satisfare
al carico che tiene della Lettura di Matematica nello Stu=
dio di Padoua,

Siriuere dauere determinato di presentare al Ser.mo Prin̄cipe
l'Ochiale et c̄ p̄ essere di giouamento inestimabile p̄ ogni
negozio et impresa marittima o terrestre stimo di tenere que=
sto nuouo artifizio nel maggior segreto et solam.te a dispositione
di S. Ser.a L'Ochiale cauato dalle piu r̄c̄ōdite speculazioni di
prospettiua ha il uantaggio di scoprire Legni et Vele dell'inimico
p̄ due hore et piu di tempo prima ch̄ egli scuopra noi et distinguendo
il numero et la qualita dei uasselli giudicare le sue forze
ballestirsi alla caccia al combattimento o alla fuga, o'pure anc̄
nella campagna aperta uedere et particularm.te distinguere ogni suo
moto et prepatamento.

Adi 7. di Gennaio
Gioue si uedde così   ♃ * oci:
Adi 8 così   ori * * ⊕ *   ♃ 10.   11.
   ♃ ⊕ * * *   era dūg diretto et nō retrogrado ori   oci:
Adi 12. si uedde in tale costituzione   * * ⊕ *
Il 13 si uededuno uicinissime à Gioue 4 stelle * ⊕ * * *   o'meglio così
Adi 14 è nugolo   * ⊕ * * *
Il 15 ⊕ * * * * * la prossa à ♃ era la minore la 4.a era di=
stante dalla 3.a il doppio circa.   ⊕ * * * *
Lo spatio delle 3 occidentali nō era   ⊕ * * *
maggiore del diametro di ♃ et e=
rano in Linea retta.   * * * ♃ Long. 71.38 Lat. 1.13

illustrations. Finding that he could see at least ten-times more stars than with the naked eye, he redrew the constellations of Orion, Taurus and the cluster of the Pleiades in detail, and added new, smaller stars which were being observed for the first time since Creation. Previously Taurus was thought to number six stars – Galileo boosted the number with a further twenty-nine. For Orion, he added seventy-one to the original nine. Observing the 'nebulous' stars of the Ptolemaic star catalogue, he was able to see that they were, in fact, made of many small stars, and deduced from this that the nebulae and the Milky Way were also 'congeries of innumerable stars grouped together in clusters', too small and far away to be resolved as separate stars by the naked eye (something that had been speculated by Aristotle).

It is easy to imagine the excitement he must have felt at being able to explore farther than any before him, especially as the discoveries kept coming. When he turned his lens towards Jupiter in January 1610, he saw that the planet moved with the company of three stars (later seen to be four), arranged in a straight line, sometimes disappearing behind the planet. These, he realized, must be satellites, and with that the four Galilean moons of Jupiter – Io, Europa, Ganymede and Callisto, their names derived from the lovers of Zeus – were documented. Galileo named them the Medician stars in dedication to his patron Cosimo II de' Medici. (Today it's known that there are actually seventy-nine moons orbiting Jupiter.) The loss of Earth's previously unique status of a planet possessing a natural satellite was another nail in the coffins of the geocentricism of the Ptolemaic and Tychonic models. Galileo scrutinized the surface of Earth's moon, which until that point was thought to be a perfectly smooth sphere. His discovery of great mountains (with his estimates of their heights) and the craters that disfigured the surface was also a revelation that was met with great excitement.

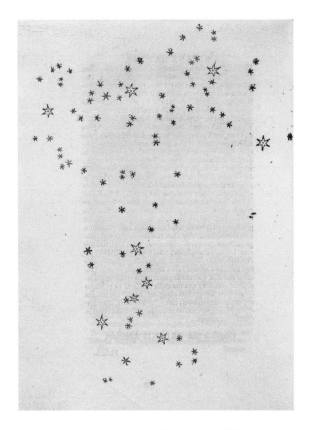

Galileo's sketch of Orion's Belt (the three bright stars at the top of the image) and surrounding stars, many of which he was the first person in history to see.

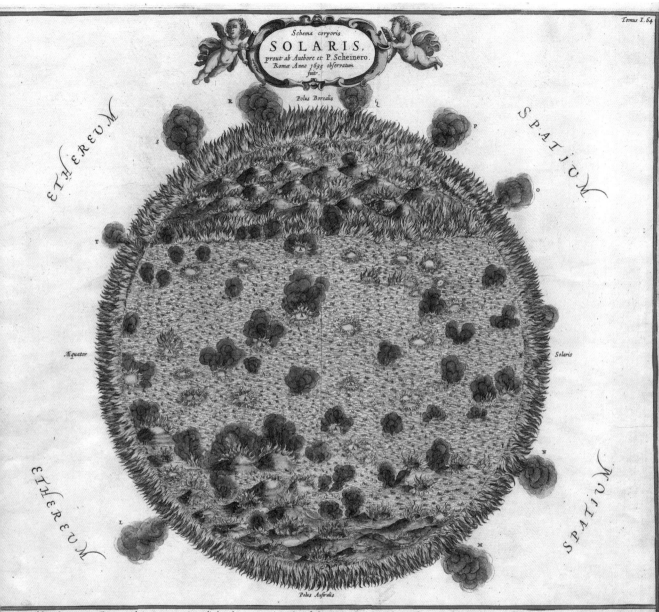

Athanasius Kircher's 1665 map of the Sun, complete with mountain ranges at its poles and a swirling solar sea at its equator. Kircher based the wonderfully strange map on the observations of sunspots made by the German Jesuit Christoph Scheiner (1573–1650), who believed that the sunspots were satellites of the Sun. In his 1612 pamphlet Three Letters on Sunspots, *Galileo controversially argues against Scheiner's thesis, stating them to be part of the Sun itself.*

After publishing these findings, Galileo continued to deliver more news of the heavens. With his *Tre lettere sulle macchie solari* ('Three Letters on Sunspots') he showed that these phenomena were not separate solar satellites, as believed, but part of the Sun itself. More significantly he showed how Venus underwent a sequence of phases similar to the Moon. This was further indictment of the Ptolemaic system, for if Venus was always between the Sun and Earth, as this belief system held, then the earthbound observer would never glimpse a Venusian 'full moon' – and yet there it was.

Galileo had taken pains to present his discoveries in an empirical manner, and temper their disruptive implications as best as he was able, for agitator status carried great risk, not least to his Medici patronage. Religious resistance to heliocentrism was based on biblical references such as Psalm 104:5: 'the Lord set the earth on its foundations; it can never be moved'; while Ecclesiastes 1:5 tells us: 'And the sun rises and sets and returns to its place.' Galileo was contradicting scripture, and, though his observations were backed by numerous Jesuit scholars, the astronomer would for years be forced to defend himself from accusations of heresy, in what is known as the Galileo Affair. This culminated in his trial and condemnation by the Roman Catholic Inquisition for his support of heliocentrism in 1633. Galileo was found 'vehemently suspect of heresy', for 'holding and defending an opinion as probable, after it has been declared contrary to Holy Scripture'. He was required to 'abjure, curse, and detest' those opinions and was sentenced to imprisonment, later commuted to house arrest, which he remained under for the rest of his life.

ABOVE: Galileo before the Holy Office, *by Joseph-Nicolas Robert-Fleury.*

OPPOSITE TOP: *The Noah's Ark constellation. In 1627, a lawyer named Julius Schiller published the star atlas* Coelum stellatum christianum, *unique in that it shows the constellations with biblical and early Christian figures, replacing the classical characters of mythology.*

OPPOSITE BOTTOM LEFT: *Galileo observed with great puzzlement Saturn's irregular form, a fluctuating shape that he described as the 'ears of Saturn'. It wasn't until 1655 that the Dutch astronomer Christiaan Huygens found that Saturn 'is surrounded by a ring, thin and flat, never touching, oblique in relation to the ecliptic'. That same year, Huygens also discovered the Saturnian moon Titan. This image is from his* Systema saturnium, *1659.*

OPPOSITE BOTTOM RIGHT: *Galileo's observations of the Moon, 1610.*

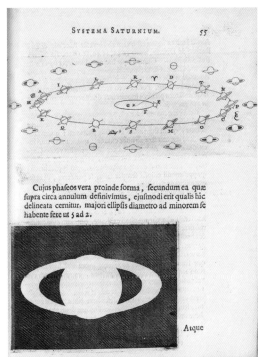

SYSTEMA SATURNIUM. 55

Cujus phaseos vera proinde forma, secundum ea quæ supra circa annulum definivimus, ejusmodi erit qualis hic delineata cernitur, majori ellipsis diametro ad minorem se habente fere ut 5 ad 2.

Atque

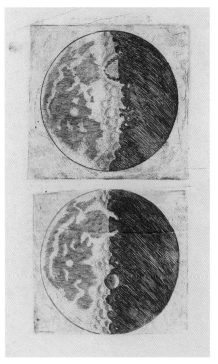

THE CARTESIAN UNIVERSE

While Galileo battled with the intellectual legacies of Aristotle and the dogma of Christian cosmic tradition, his younger contemporary, the French philosopher and mathematician René Descartes (1596–1650) decided to jettison the ancient Greek writings in favour of his own systematic search for the foundation of absolute truth. Descartes's quest for certainty meant starting from scratch, resetting to a default position of indiscriminate doubt until one is left only with the undeniable. His own existence passed the test, for he thought, therefore he

A 1769 collection of astronomical instruments, world map and the cosmic systems of Copernicus, Brahe and, in the bottom-right corner of the top-centre image, Descartes.

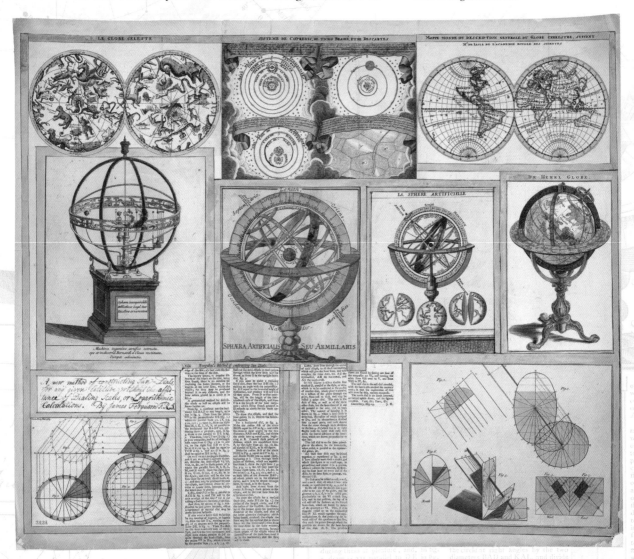

was: 'We cannot doubt of our existence while we doubt.' A devout Catholic, the existence of God was proven to Descartes by the very thought of such a perfect being, which could not possibly have originated in Descartes's own flawed mortal mind. 'Of all the ideas that are in me, the idea that I have of God is the most true, the most clear and distinct', he wrote in *Meditationes de prima philosophia* ('Meditations on First Philosophy') in 1641.

But what of the cosmos? The notion of a vacuum had not yet been conceived. Instead Descartes suggested the opposite – a plenum. His was a universe packed full of elements that had emerged from total chaos. Its particles swirled together in a circular motion in great vortices, obeying a set of his stated laws of motion. When one particle moved, its neighbour took its place. This led to the mind-boggling idea that space and matter were, therefore, essentially one and the same, even though matter could move through space.

René Descartes.

This is what gave the planets their rotational orbits on such long and distant paths because – like boats that hit the riverbank at a sudden bend in the river – their weight carried them out farther from the lighter surrounding particles, which were unable to sway their course. In the Aristotelian universe, and subsequent models, the celestial bodies were separate existing objects, each moving in accordance with their own nature. In the Cartesian universe, however, the planets were *defined* by motion, the universe like a giant swirling sand pit of endless movement. It was – is – a truly extraordinary idea (and again one that is perhaps best understood with the aid of the images that accompanied Descartes's original presentation of the idea – see images overleaf). Significantly, the idea of these vortices throughout the universe also raised the idea that the fixed stars were Suns of their own systems, buffeting against each other and our own. This would be an idea of great influence on future cosmology.

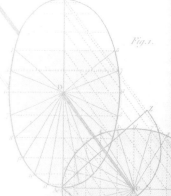

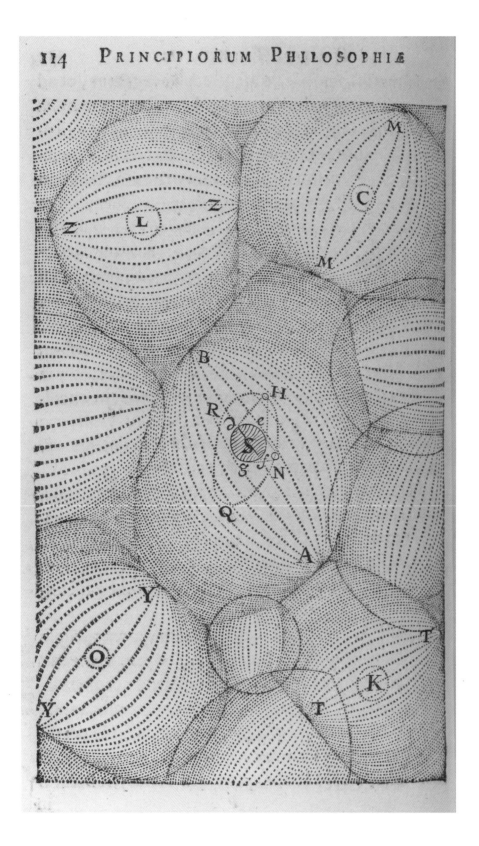

LEFT: *The vortices that make up the Cartesian universe. The Sun, made of lighter elements, remains at the centre, while planets of heavier particles are sifted out and circle around it, farther out.*

OPPOSITE: *This diagram of the Cartesian vortices is used by Descartes to illustrate his theory of how the vortex around a dying star (here represented by 'N') would collapse, leading to the star being drawn into the neighbouring vortex. Should it remain there, it became a planet; but if it moved onto another vortex it became a comet. Descartes's comets are, therefore, linear-path journeyers, a conceit that would be refuted by the identified return of Halley's Comet in 1758, which was used to disprove his ideas.*

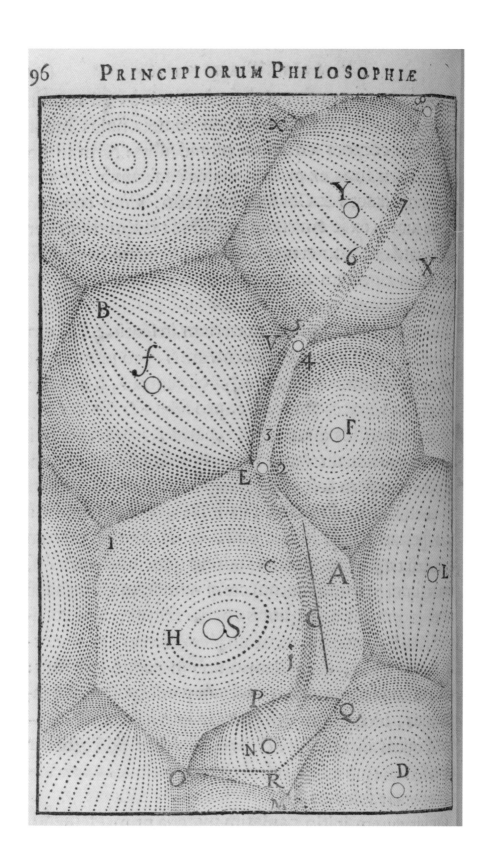

JOHANNES HEVELIUS
MAPS THE MOON

It was a coachman's candle that started the blaze on 26
September 1679, the flames tearing through the stables to
engulf the adjoining Stellaburgum ('Star-castle') Observatory
and destroying, with tragic irony, the work of a man who
had spent forty years recording the fires of distant stars. The
observatory of Johannes Hevelius (1611–1687) was Europe's
finest, built by the astronomer himself in Danzig (now Gdańsk,
Poland) before those at Greenwich and Paris were even in the
planning stage. Though a handful of his books were rescued
before the building collapsed, the bulk of his data and the

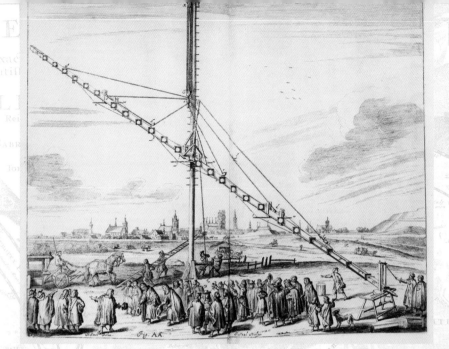

instruments he had built by hand were lost. Faced with this crushing misfortune, at a whitened age of sixty-eight, Hevelius saw only one option: he immediately began to rebuild.

The founder of lunar topography and discoverer of constellations came from a family of brewing merchants, but after observing the solar eclipse on 1 June 1639 Hevelius had been inspired to abandon the family business and had dedicated himself completely to astronomy. In 1641 Hevelius had pieced together an observatory along the roofs of his three linked houses, equipping it with elaborate instruments that eventually featured a telescope based on the 1611 design of Johannes Kepler. An improvement on Galileo's design, a Keplerian telescope used a convex, not concave, lens as the eyepiece, which provided a much wider field of view and allowed much higher magnification. To facilitate this, the length of the tube needed to be considerable. When completed, Hevelius's invention had grown to a massive length of 150ft (46m), likely the longest ever built before the introduction of 'tubeless' aerial telescopes.

By 1647 the brewer–astronomer had produced the first lunar atlas, *Selenographia*, mapping every observable detail of the Moon's surface. He engraved the illustrations himself, and produced it with a printing press in his observatory. One of the charts of the full Moon was even made into a working volvelle (a rotatable disc with a measuring string that was used to turn the Moon to match its orientation). The work brought him near instant fame across Europe.

Hevelius publicly demonstrating his enormous 150ft- (46m-) long telescope, 1641, from his Machinae coelestis *('Heavenly Machine').*

OPPOSITE: *Johann Doppelmayr's double-hemisphere map of the Moon, first issued in 1707. The work is based on the 1647 observations of brewer and astronomer Johannes Hevelius and those of the Italian astronomer Giovanni Battista Riccioli, who originated many of the names of lunar features in use today (such as the Mare Tranquillitatis, 'Sea of Tranquillity', site of the Apollo 11 landing in 1969).*

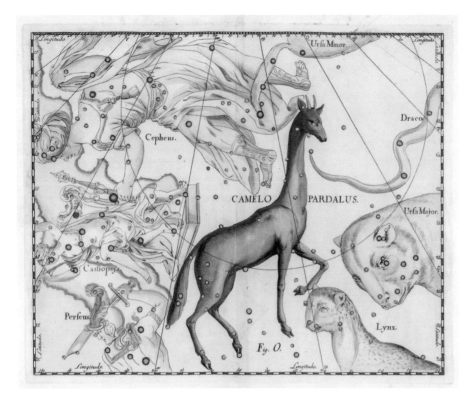

A chart of the Camelopardalis constellation by Hevelius, 1687.

Hevelius's map of the Cygnus (Swan) constellation.

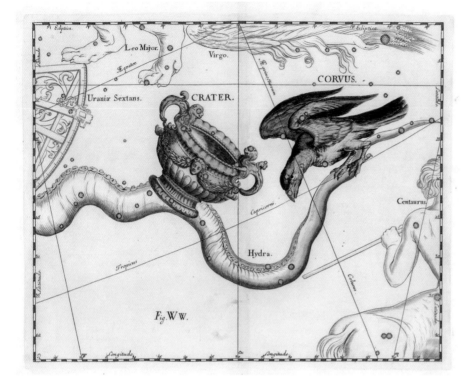

The Hydra constellation.

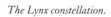

The Lynx constellation.

'He hath Made above thirty large mappes, prints, or Copper peeces of the Manner of every daies encrease and decrease', wrote the English traveller Peter Mundy admiringly in his diary, 'deciphering in her land and sea, Mountaines, valleies, Ilands, lakes, etts., making in another little world, giving Names to every part, as wee in a mappe of our world.'

Hevelius inherited the family brewery in 1649, but despite the responsibilities that came with this and his role as a town councillor, he continued with his obsessive sky-gazing. Between 1652 and 1677 his discoveries included four new comets (which led to his theory that these celestial objects revolve around the Sun in parabolic paths) and ten new constellations, seven of which remain recognized today. His most pleasing finding, though, was that his fascination with astronomy was shared by his young second wife Elisabeth. Together the couple carefully recorded the locations of the constellations. Their work demonstrated the constantly shifting nature of the cosmos, and helped to cement the still untrusted concept of a heliocentric universe.

ABOVE: *A 1651 celestial chart of the southern hemisphere by Antoine de Fer. Curiously it was designed to be printed in a mirror image, perhaps to allow the study of its astrology in secret.*

BELOW: *Johannes and Elisabeth Hevelius performing observations together.*

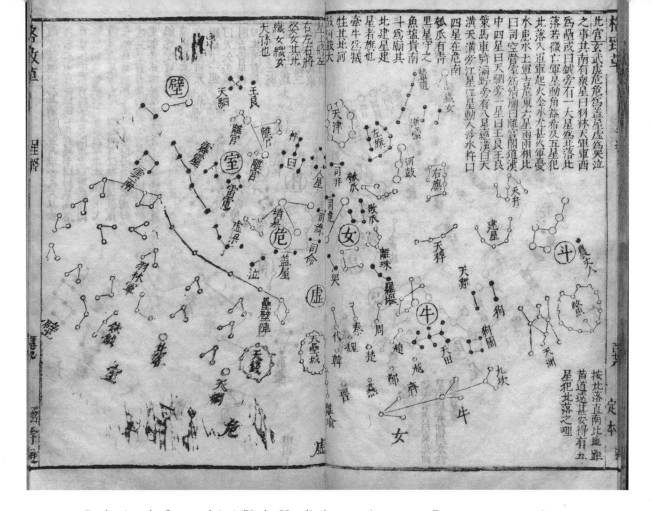

By the time the fire struck in 1679, the Hevelius's reputation was such that his appeal to the French king Louis XIV for financial aid to rebuild his observatory was instantly granted (helped by the astronomer's reminder, in a letter to the monarch, that 'I have set in the Heavens nigh to seven hundred Stars which were not there aforetimes, and have named some of them after your Majesty').

Hevelius writes of Elisabeth as being the 'faithful Aide of my nocturnal Observations', and after his death in 1687 she continued the work alone, eventually publishing their studies in *Prodromus astronomiae* (1690), a catalogue of 1564 stars. Elisabeth's achievements are all the more remarkable when one considers the time in which they were produced, when female involvement in such study was unprecedented. As such, Elisabeth is celebrated as the first female astronomer; while the greatest testaments to Johannes's genius are the fact that his lunar maps were used as the standard for more than a century, with many of his stellar discoveries remaining recognized to this day.

For contemporary comparison: a Chinese chart of constellations and asterisms published in 1648. Xiong Mingyu's work Ge zhi cao ('A Draft on Investigation of Things') discusses the heavenly motions, Moon and stars, displaying a familiarity with Western principles.

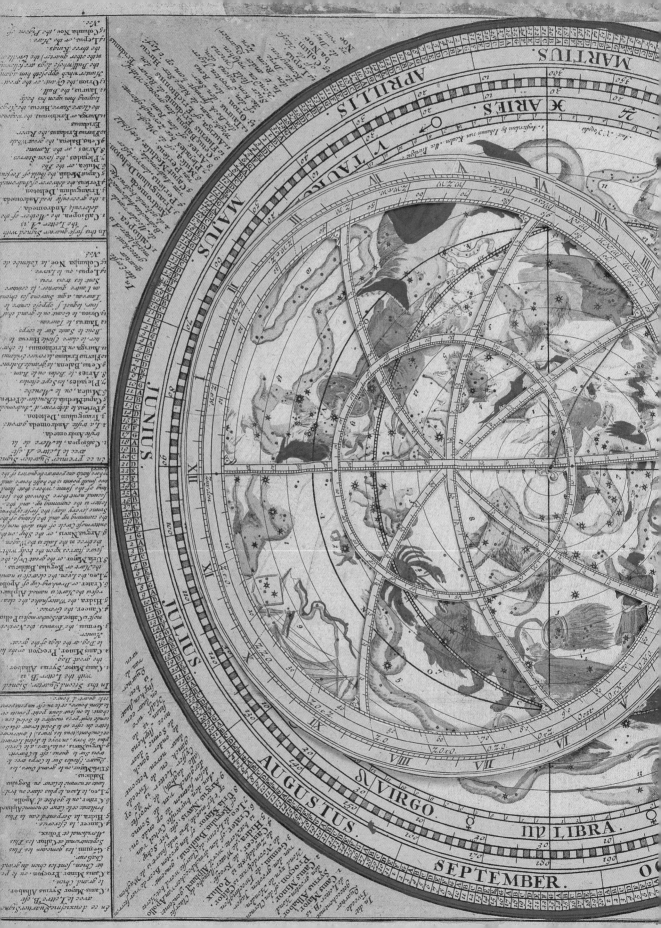

A large celestial chart by Claes Jansz Vooght of Amsterdam with a printed volvelle (turning paper ring) for performing astronomical calculations, c.1680.

SITVS
CIRCVLIS
CIRCVN:

ZENITH

NADIR.

G. van Loon f.

Situs terrae circulis coelestibus…, *a map of the Ptolemaic system from Andreas Cellarius's* Harmonia macrocosmica. *Published in 1660 by Jan Janssonius, the book is commonly agreed to be the most beautiful star atlas ever made.*

NEWTONIAN PHYSICS

Among the young intellectuals of Paris and Cambridge, the iconoclasm of Descartes's vortices had stirred up great excitement. As thrilling as the new explanation was, ostensibly explaining the observable positions of the planets at that moment, Descartes's system provided no help to the astronomer in predicting celestial behaviour. Descartes's cosmos was one of chaos, with bodies travelling with unforeseeable behaviour.

The mystery that remained for astronomers of the mid-seventeenth century was the force that drove planetary movement. Kepler believed that, whatever this force was, it emanated from the Sun, the 'soul' of the universe, which bore similarity to Descartes's torrid matter-filled system, where the celestial bodies were swept around on elliptical paths by a giant central solar vortex. Other theories were also in circulation. Kepler himself had been influenced by the work of the English physician William Gilbert, who in 1600 had published *De magnete...* ('On the Magnet...') in which he stated the theory that Earth was a giant attractive magnet. This explained the fall of objects back to the ground, and the behaviour of the magnetic compass.

The subject of planetary movement, the trajectories of comets and Earth's magnetic draw had been of much discussion at the Royal Society since its founding in 1660. In 1674 its curator of experiments, the prolific genius Robert Hooke (1635–1703) published his tremendously important 'suppositions', approaching the idea of gravity as we know it today as universal attraction. The first supposition proposed that celestial bodies (including Earth) possessed an attraction affecting not only their own parts but also other celestial bodies. The second stated that all bodies put into a direct and simple motion 'will so continue to move forward in a straight line, till they are by some other effectual powers deflected and bent into a Motion, describing a Circle, Ellipsis or some other more compounded Curve Line'. The third stated that the pulling power depended on 'how much nearer the body wrought on is to their own Centers'. With the second supposition, Hooke had published the first true description

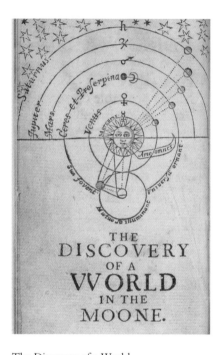

The Discovery of a World in the Moone *(1638) by John Wilkins, in which the natural philosopher and founding member of the Royal Society discusses the possibility of journeying to the Moon if the traveller could escape the supposed magnetic draw of Earth, first suggested by William Gilbert.*

OPPOSITE: *Detail from* Entretiens sur la pluralité des mondes *('Discussions on the Plurality of Worlds') by Bernard Le Bovier de Fontenelle, 1686, which explains the Copernican world system and the mechanistic physics of Descartes in elegant dialogues between a philosopher and a lady.*

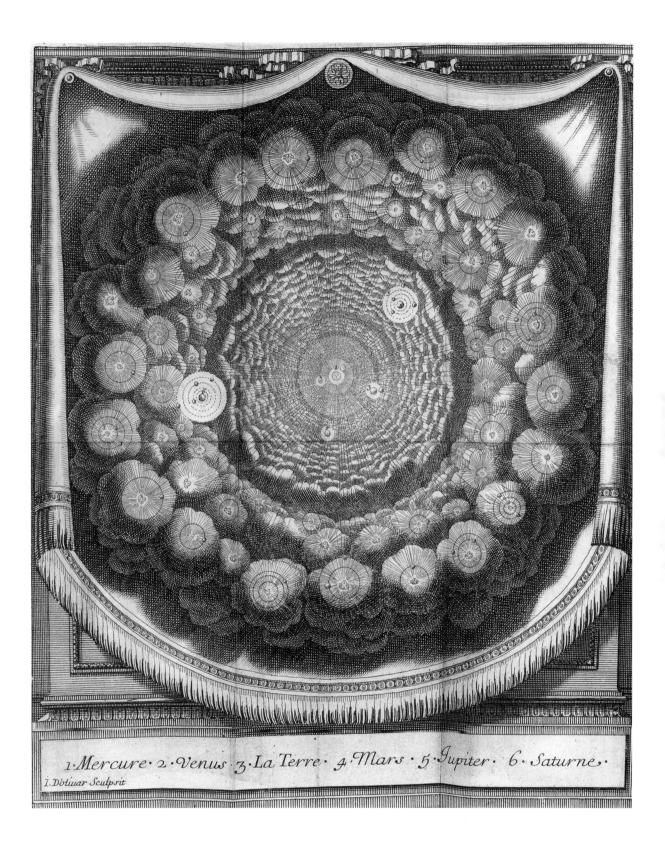

1. Mercure . 2. Venus . 3. La Terre . 4. Mars . 5. Jupiter . 6. Saturne .

I. Döliwar Sculpsit

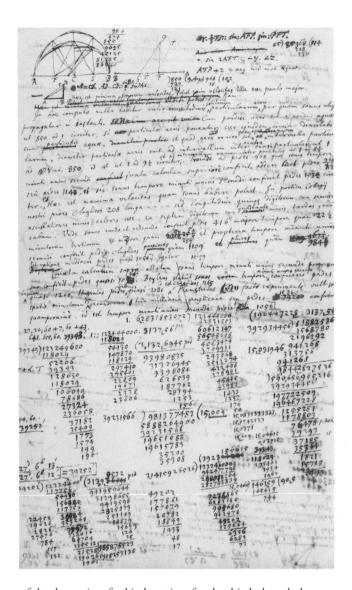

A page from Isaac Newton's notes on the Principia.

of the dynamics of orbital motion; for the third, though, he needed a precise formula to calculate just how the attraction of a body increased or diminished in relation to the distance to the object that was subjected to its draw.

For this Hooke settled on the 'inverse-square' law (that the intensity is inversely proportional to the square of the distance from the source) and wrote to Isaac Newton (1642–1727) at Cambridge with his proposal. Newton was, at this time, a Cartesian, wrestling with the problems presented by the vortices, and so was intrigued by Hooke's suggestion. Following a correspondence with Hooke in the winter of 1679–1680, he set about solving the problem.

Following a conversation in January 1684 with Sir Christopher Wren (1632–1723) and Robert Hooke, Edmond Halley (1656–1742) went to visit Newton in Cambridge. According to the mathematician Abraham de Moivre, Halley asked him 'what he thought the curve would be that would be described by the planets supposing the force of attraction towards the Sun to be reciprocal to the square of their distance from it'. Newton replied that it would be an ellipse. How did he know? 'Why… I have calculated it.'

The modest packet of nine pages that Newton first sent to Halley as proof was an early drafting of hypotheses and calculations that he would eventually publish in 1687 as *Philosophiæ naturalis principia mathematica*, a three-volume work and one of the most important in the history of science, commonly referred to as the *Principia*.* The challenge of deciphering the myriad moving parts of celestial mathematics with this new key 'exceeds', commented Newton, 'if I am not mistaken, the force of any human mind'. Gone was the crammed, tangible plenum of Descartes; in its place was empty space, punctured with the periodic journeys of celestial bodies that subjected – and, equally, were subjected to – an attractive force. Newton investigated an idea first suggested by Hooke: that this inverse-square law of attraction was true of all bodies of matter regardless of size, from a stone to a planet, that the effect diminished only with distance. The notion that, for example, two equal-sized objects of matter, at equal distance from the Moon, with one buried deep beneath the earth, could exert the same amount of pull on the Moon would be so alien to even followers of Newton for years to come that some pointed to God as the cause. But as Newton worked through the idea, he was eventually able to show successfully that Earth's pull on the Moon was what brought it out of a linear path and into our planet's orbit, just as Earth drew a falling stone back to its surface with the same attractive force.

Newton's original treatise expanded rapidly with stunning new discoveries. The tides? These were the result of this draw of both the Moon and the Sun. The precession of the

*At one point, publication of the great work almost stalled because of a critical lack of funds. The Royal Society was reluctant, as it had just lost a huge amount of money publishing an unpopular illustrated book called *De historia piscium* ('The History of Fish') by Francis Willughby, and so Halley offered to finance the *Principia* himself. The Society agreed, but told Halley that it also couldn't afford to pay his £50 salary – so he was paid in unsold copies of *De historia piscium*.

Sir Isaac Newton, 1689.

equinoxes, puzzled over since Hipparchus (see the Heavenly Spheres entry on page 59), were explained by the spinning Earth bulging at its equator and being flatter at its poles, which would cause it to teeter in its rotation, again caused by gravitation. (Newton's original precession equations did not quite work, however, and were later corrected by Jean le Rond d'Alembert in 1749.) The new law of attraction also allowed Newton to calculate the mass of those planets that possessed moons, by studying the behaviour of the satellites. This led to the realization that Jupiter and Saturn were giants that dwarfed Earth, but the stability of the solar system was maintained by their relatively distant positions from the Sun (with the occasional intervention of God also thought to be a contributing factor). To the stars, however, Newton paid little attention.* There was no evidence to suggest that – relative to

*Newton did, however, make the first noted observation of the 'starbursts' of light visible when one rubs one's own eyes. Today these are called phosphenes (light particles created by cells in the eye when under pressure). The crew of the Apollo 11 mission all experienced the phenomenon, though each decided not to mention it to the others for fear of being thought ill. (A directly related phenomena is 'Prisoner's cinema', reported by prison inmates when left in the dark for extended periods.)

*Engraving by John Faber of the
astronomer Edmond Halley.*

each other – they moved at all, no reason to dispute the ancient
Greek assertion of the 'fixed' stars. In fact in the *Principia*
Newton uses the Latin term 'fixa' (as in *stella fixa*) for star.

Where the Cartesian system appealed in its relative ease of
understanding, with philosophical language and a physical
framework of infinite cosmic collisions, Newton's Principia
was built on complex mathematics, and the far more difficult
idea of an invisible force that he could not explain, but merely
point to its effects as proof of existence. It took some time to be
accepted and absorbed into mainstream knowledge. Any doubt
of its correctness, however, would be resolved in 1758 when a
comet appeared in the sky, because for the first time in human
history it was expected. Its reappearance had been predicted
accurately by Edmond Halley in 1705, using Newtonian laws.

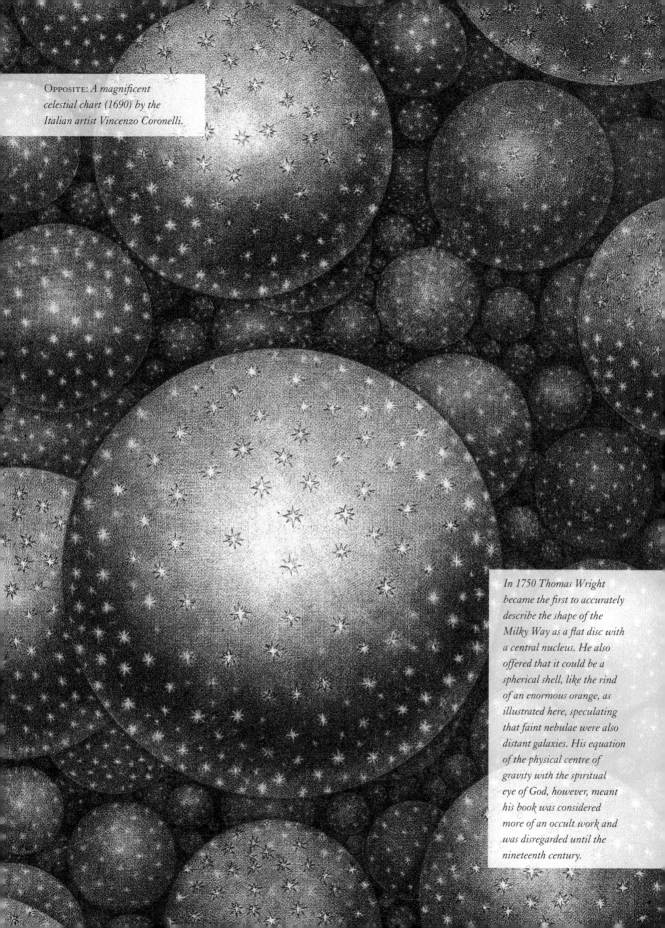

In 1750 Thomas Wright became the first to accurately describe the shape of the Milky Way as a flat disc with a central nucleus. He also offered that it could be a spherical shell, like the rind of an enormous orange, as illustrated here, speculating that faint nebulae were also distant galaxies. His equation of the physical centre of gravity with the spiritual eye of God, however, meant his book was considered more of an occult work and was disregarded until the nineteenth century.

HALLEY'S COMET

It was Edmond Halley's coaxing that had convinced Newton to publish *Philosophiæ naturalis principia mathematica*. In it Newton had theorized that comets obeyed the same law of inverse-square attraction: they too were prisoners of the Sun's gravity (unless they possessed a velocity of sufficient rate to escape), but as they travelled at greater speeds their paths would be of a much more elongated ellipsis than the almost circular orbits of the planets. This was at odds with previous beliefs, including those of Hooke, who had essentially dismissed comets as being beyond the influence of attraction. When a comet had been spotted travelling towards the Sun in November 1680, and another moving in the opposite direction in December, John Flamsteed, Astronomer Royal at the Greenwich Observatory, had made the groundbreaking suggestion that they were the same comet (which indeed

Celestial models illustrating the blazing comet of March and April 1742, by Matthaus Seutter.

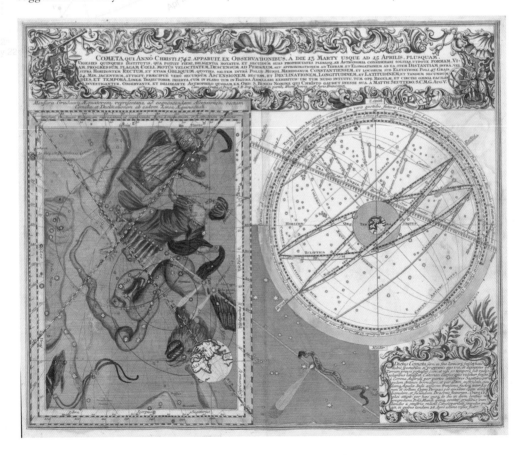

they were). His explanation, however, was wide of the mark, coming to the Cartesian conclusion that the comet had been drawn in by the giant solar vortex and then repelled like an opposing magnet by the Sun back on an outward journey. Newton, however, believed it more likely that the comet had

The 1066 appearance of Halley's Comet (centre, top) depicted in the Bayeux tapestry.

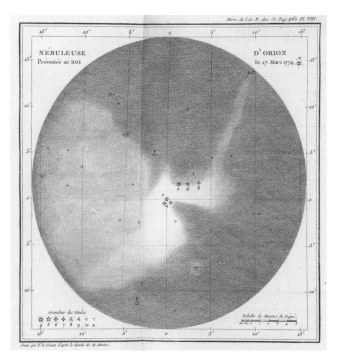

The Orion Nebula as drawn by Charles Messier (1730–1817). From the rickety roof of the Hôtel de Cluny in downtown Paris, the amateur French comet hunter recorded a catalogue of more than 100 'deep sky objects' he observed with his 4in (10cm) telescope for three years from 1753. Though Messier made the list out of frustration, to avoid recording the objects again (he was solely interested in comets), his accidental discoveries became of great importance, and included spectacular examples of diffuse nebulae, planetary nebulae, open clusters, globular clusters and galaxies. Messier's catalogue of deep-sky objects has been heavily studied ever since.

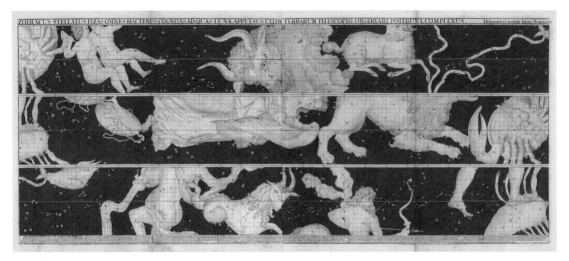

'fetched a compass' about the Sun, that is, that it had travelled around the back of the Sun and was then catapulted along its return elliptical path.

Halley obsessed over the idea that some comets could be periodic visitors travelling in elliptical orbits, and realized that the proof of this, and of Newtonian science, would be to find patterns among records of historical comet appearances. And so he set about compiling centuries of sightings, searching for

ABOVE: The Zodiacus stellatus... *c.1746 was created by Halley, based on the observations of John Flamsteed, Royal Astronomer at the Greenwich Observatory, who had given his permission for only the text of his catalogue to be published.*

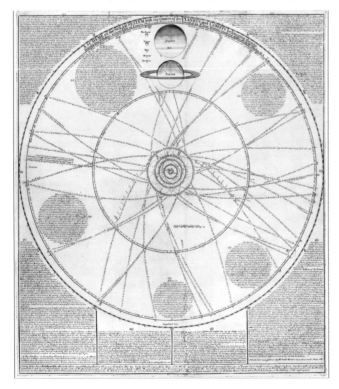

LEFT: A Scheme of the Solar System with the Orbits of the Planets and Comets belonging thereto... *by William Whiston, based on Halley's table of comets. The English theologian believed comets responsible for the Great Flood and other past disasters in human history. Comets were populated and served as 'so many hells for tormenting the damned with perpetual vicissitudes of heat and cold'.*

In 1750 the French astronomer Nicolas-Louis de Lacaille (1713–1762) travelled to the Cape of Good Hope to compile the first comprehensive catalogue of more than 10,000 stars of the southern hemisphere, and determine the distances of the planets trigonometrically. We find his work added to later maps, including this 1787 chart by Johann Elert Bode (1747–1826), which features new de Lacaille constellations the Sculptor's Workshop and the Pneumatic Pump (the latter a recent invention).

events that could be attributed to the same cosmic journeyer. The comet of 1682 stood out, along with those of 1607 and 1531, as all shared a retrograde path (i.e. moving in opposite direction to the planets), with a similar interval of 75–76 years. The lack of precision was a problem, until Halley realized that this could be accounted for by the comet falling under the influence of the various planets it passed, altering its path but never diverting its essential circuit. If he was right, then the comet would next appear 'about the end of the year 1758, or the beginning of the next', he predicted.

As this date of Halley's prediction approached, there was great excitement* that an astronomical forecast could be proved right with such a dramatic celestial display; and also a little trepidation in those who still held the ominous association of a comet's appearance. Would there be a delay caused by unforeseen planetary influence? Halley had anticipated this in part, but had neglected to account for the pull of Jupiter on the comet's earlier outward journey away from the Sun. However,

Carte de l'hémisphère boreal… *by Charles Messier, from* Mémoires de l'Académie royale des sciences*, 1760. This map was the instrument used to identify Halley's Comet.*

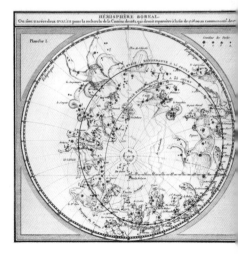

*Though not nearly as much excitement of the terrified kind that greeted Halley's Comet when it reappeared in 1910. In 1881, the British astronomer Sir William Huggins had discovered that the tails of comets contain cyanogen, a kind of cyanide; and on 7 February 1910 the *New York Times* falsely reported that astronomers around the world were now concerned that Halley's Comet, which was due to pass between the Earth and the Sun, would spray the Earth with poison gas. The article caused international panic.

this had been noted by the French astronomer Alexis Claude Clairaut (1713–1765), and together with Nicole-Reine Lepaute (1723–1788) – one of the few women working officially in the field of astronomy at this time – and Jérôme Lalande (1732–1807), Halley's figures were refined, with a more specific prediction of a perihelion passage of April 1759. Both forecasts of Halley and the French were good: the comet was first sighted by Johann Georg Palitzsch (1723–1788), a German farmer and astronomer, on Christmas Day 1758. It eventually passed through its perihelion (the point at which a travelling body

FOLLOWING PAGES: *A hand-drawn Indian star map created in Rajasthan, c.1780, showing the northern and southern celestial hemispheres. The constellations of antiquity, as listed by Ptolemy, are decorated in gold. Ptolemaic astronomy maintained an influence in Indian astronomy long after the scientific revolution of sixteenth-century Europe; these manuscript star charts were produced until the late nineteenth century for predominantly astrological purposes.*

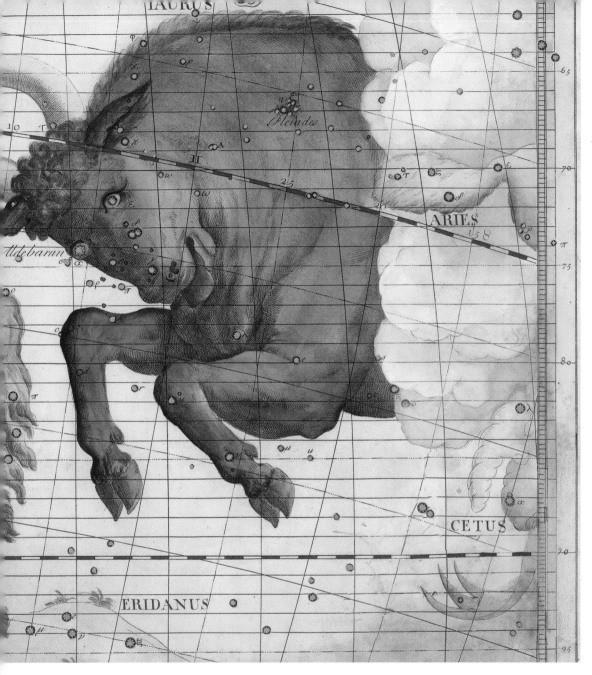

is closest to the Sun) on 13 March 1759. (The attraction of Jupiter and Saturn had caused a delay of 618 days.) This was the same comet recorded by Petrus Apianus in 1531, the one observed by Johannes Kepler in 1607 and, in fact, the same observed by Babylonian astronomers in 164 BC and by Chinese astronomers in 240 BC. With his Synopsis of the *Astronomy of Comets* (1705), Halley had been the first to prove that the appearance of comets can be periodic, but sadly he died in 1742, too soon to see the spectacular confirmation of both his calculations, and the laws of Newton's science.

ABOVE: *The* Atlas coelestis *by John Flamsteed, published in 1729, is one of the most beautiful star atlases ever created. Here he depicts the Taurus and Orion constellations.*

THE MOD

Following Edmond Halley's successful demonstration (see Halley's Comet entry on pages 164-167), Newtonian science gathered acceptance in the middle of the eighteenth century. With the aid of increasingly powerful telescopes, preoccupation with the precise positioning and classification of heavenly bodies was at its peak. But, with the nineteenth century, a new obsession rose to the fore, driven by the latest developments in chemistry, physics, mathematics and geology. Greater understanding of the composition of Earth offered greater understanding of the makeup of stars, comets and planets. But how to test the untouchable?

ERN SKY

'Equipped with his five senses, man explores the universe around him and calls the adventure Science.'

Edwin Hubble

*System of the Interior or Empyrean Heaven,
Shewing the fall of Lucifer.*

Dodd delin.   Prattent sculp.

LEFT: *While science was providing sophisticated solutions, theories of the occult also maintained a popularity. The astrologer Ebenezer Sibly offered an alternative vision of the sky with his 1794 map* System of the Interior or Empyrean Heaven, Shewing the Fall of Lucifer.

OPPOSITE: *A nineteenth-century Mongolian book of astrology. The manuscript features dozens of charts used by Buddhist monks to calculate calendars of auspicious days and to predict astronomical events. The text is written in Tibetan, and closely follows the traditions of works such as the Kalachakra Tantra (1024), important to Buddhist cosmology.*

All the necessary data, it would emerge, was carried by light. The invention of spectroscopy allowed the identification of chemical components of light-radiating bodies, by dispersing the light according to its wavelength with a prism. This would ultimately usher in a new branch of astronomy: astrophysics – a revolution in sky science. Poetically, the late eighteenth-century figure whose many significant achievements included his instrumental role in the investigation of this starlight harmony was by training not an astronomer but a musician – William Herschel.

FOLLOWING PAGES: Aurora Borealis *by Frederic Church, 1865. The painting alludes to the fact that, during the American Civil War, the aurora was widely interpreted as an omen indicating God's anger with the Confederacy for advocating slavery, and the importance of a Union victory.*

WILLIAM AND CAROLINE HERSCHEL

Before making the discoveries in Britain that earned him
consideration as one of the greatest astronomers in history,
William Herschel (1738–1832) had been a German refugee.
After the victory of the Kingdom of France in the Seven
Years' War in 1763, in which his homeland of Hanover had
fought for the opposing British coalition, Herschel had fled to
England. A trained musician, his fortunes improved when he
was appointed organist at the Octagon Chapel in Bath, and
with new financial security was able to explore other interests.
Chief among these was astronomy, which he developed by
devouring books such as Robert Smith's *A Compleat System*

William and Caroline Herschel
working on a telescope mirror.

of *Opticks* in (1738), and *Astronomy Explained upon Sir Isaac Newton's Principles* (1756) – the latter a useful 'translation' of the science for those not mathematically trained. With the desire to see the sights mentioned in these books, and those that lay farther, Herschel started building his own reflecting telescope. He rejected the more popular but expensive lenses of refractive telescopes – they simply could not offer the power he sought. Instead he started building his own reflective models, which used curved mirrors.

Having ground and polished his own mirrors,* by 4 March 1774 Herschel was, in partnership with his sister Caroline (1750–1848), observing the Orion Nebula with his own 5½ft- (1.6m-) focal-length device. Right away, as he recorded in his diary, he noticed that, in comparison with Robert Smith's illustrations, the nebula had visibly changed shape. Nebulae at this time had been observed only as faint, milky shapes (nebula is derived from the Latin word for mist), and no discovery had been made of their composition, though it was thought that they were perhaps composed of a radiant ethereal fluid 'that shines with its own proper lustre', according to Edmond Halley. Herschel made the startling discovery that they could change shape, that 'there are undoubtedly changes among the fixt Stars', and he was spurred on to unravel this and other mysteries found in his and Caroline's night watching.

The spiral galaxy NGC 2683, nicknamed the UFO galaxy for its flying-saucer shape. It was discovered by William Herschel on 5 February 1788, in the northern constellation of Lynx. (This constellation, incidentally, was named not because it had any feline resemblance, but because its faintness required the sensitive eyes of a cat to discern it.)

*Herschel, who built more than 400 telescopes, cast all his own mirrors in iron, heated in a wood and coal furnace. His chosen material for the mould was slightly more unusual; after a variety of trials, he found that the best substance was pounded horse dung. Surprisingly the use of horse-dung moulds continued into the twentieth century, incorporated, for example, by the St Gobain glassworks, Paris, in their crafting of the 100in (2.5m) mirror for the Mount Wilson Observatory's Hooker telescope, completed in 1917.

By 1781 Herschel had upgraded to a 7ft (2.1m) reflector, and during a routine observation of the constellation Gemini in March he noticed that an object previously thought to be a star was in fact a 'wanderer' – one that we now know as Uranus. He had become the first person in recorded history to discover a new planet. At first Herschel assumed it to be a comet, and notified Nevil Maskelyne, the Astronomer Royal, whose inferior equipment meant he was unable to see the object. After confirmation of its planetary nature from the Russian academic Anders Johan Lexell, Herschel named it Georgium sidus ('Georgian star') after King George III, but it quickly became known as Uranus, to Herschel's chagrin. (Johann Bode later discovered that Tobias Mayer had marked the object in 1756, as had John Flamsteed in 1690 – both had assumed it a star.) The discovery earned Herschel the position of Astronomer to the King. With the accompanying pension and income from the manufacture of telescopes, the Herschels were able to dedicate all their time to scanning the skies.

Later in 1781, armed with a giant 20ft (6m) telescope with 18in- (45cm-) diameter mirrors, Herschel returned to the mystery of the nebulae and began to sweep the entire English sky in search of the phenomena. He was armed with the

An example of a ghost constellation. The Telescopium Herschelii (shown on this 1825 map as the telescope below the Lynx) constellation was established by the astronomer Maximilian Hell in honour of Herschel's discovery of Uranus but fell out of use by the nineteenth century.

In 1766 Henry Cavendish had discovered hydrogen gas, naming it 'flammable air', but he is arguably most famous for the publishing of his experiment to determine the density of Earth, from which this diagram of the apparatus used is taken. The design was based on the work of his friend John Michell, who most remarkably theorized the existence of black holes in 1783, which he called 'dark stars', suggesting that such a star of a diameter 500 times the Sun would be so massive that its gravitational pull would prevent its light from escaping, rendering it invisible.

catalogue produced by Charles Messier (see Halley's Comet entry on page 165), which collected sixty-eight nebulae, clusters and galaxies. For the next twenty years the Herschels used their powerful instruments to methodically scour every square inch of their sky, aided from 1789 with a larger 40ft (12m) telescope.

Caroline's role in William's success, and the discoveries she made in her own right, are often omitted. Over the course of her sky-gazing career with her brother, Caroline Herschel, the first woman to discover a comet, would find more than 2400 astronomical objects. This was especially remarkable given her inauspicious beginnings: left blind in one eye and 4ft 3in (1.3m) tall after a childhood bout of typhus, she was forced to consult multiplication tables while she worked, for as a woman she had been forbidden from learning mathematics. She began by documenting her brother's work, but finding John Flamsteed's catalogue inconveniently organized by constellation she created her own star catalogue organized by North Polar distance, a task she labelled 'minding the heavens'. For verification, she also swept the skies herself. On 26 February 1783, she discovered a nebula not marked in the Messier catalogue; that same year she found another two. At this, William immediately began his own search for nebulae, and Caroline was, reluctantly, relegated to documenting his observations. 'It was not til the last two months of the same year', she wrote, 'before I felt the least encouragement for spending the starlight nights on a grass-plot covered with dew or hoar frost without a human being near enough to be within call.'

An illustration of nebulae by William Herschel.

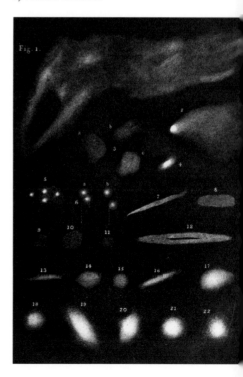

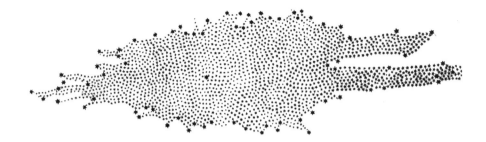

*William Herschel's sketch
of the Milky Way.*

Between 1786 and 1797, Caroline discovered eight comets,
five of which were published in the journal of the Royal
Society. The first seven comets were found using a telescope
her brother had built for her, but her eighth and final comet
discovery, on 6 August 1797, she made with her naked
eye. She immediately rode the 30 miles (48km) or so to the
observatory in Greenwich to tell the Astronomer Royal, Nevil
Maskelyne. She became the first woman to receive a salary for
scientific endeavours, at a time when men were rarely paid
for such pursuits, and she was honoured with a gold medal
and honorary membership of the Royal Astronomical Society,
as well as honorary membership of the Royal Irish Academy,
and the Gold Medal of Science from the King of Prussia.
Remarkably two of the catalogues she created are still in use,
and the lunar crater C. Herschel on the west side of Mare
Imbrium is named in her memory.

By 1802 the Herschels had together trumped Messier's
number of observed nebulae by documenting an astonishing
sum of 2500. In 1820 they published a catalogue of 5000. But
of what, exactly, were these luminous pools of celestial mist
composed? Through his enormously powerful scope, Herschel
decided that some nebulae, marked by dark colour variations,
were dense clusters of stars, while the other, milkier variety
were 'true' nebulae, that is, composed of glowing fluid. Almost
immediately after this theory was announced at the Royal
Society in June 1784, Herschel realized he was wrong. The
milky nebulosity was the result of greater distance – all nebulae
were clusters of stars.

In 1785 he published his re-envisioning of the galaxy and
its origins in *On the Construction of the Heavens*. Stars were
originally scattered uniformly, and gradually clustered together
under the influence of gravitational attraction. This would
later chime perfectly with the conclusions of the French
astronomer Pierre-Simon, marquis de Laplace (1749–1827),
published in 1796 in *Exposition du Système du Monde* ('The

OPPOSITE: *A Chinese celestial map
that combines the European
ecliptic coordinate system and the
Chinese equatorial system, 1821.
Star locations are provided in the
form of poetry.*

System of the World'). Laplace proposed the origin story of there having been a giant nebula swirling around the Sun, from which the stars and planets condensed. (Laplace's 'nebula hypothesis' also explained why the planets moved in the same direction around the Sun.) Herschel refined his view of nebulosity in 1790, following the sighting of 'a most singular phaenomenon' – a bright star with a faint luminous atmosphere. He was witnessing, he thought, the birth of a star, condensing from a diffuse cloud of nebulosity. He revised his idea of the galaxy with the reintroduction of nebulosity. The Orion Nebula, previously thought to be so far beyond (and indeed larger than) our galaxy that its stars were impossible to see, was repositioned within the Milky Way. Ours was now a galaxy 'the most brilliant, and beyond all comparison the most extensive sidereal system'.

William Herschel's 20ft (6m) reflecting telescope.

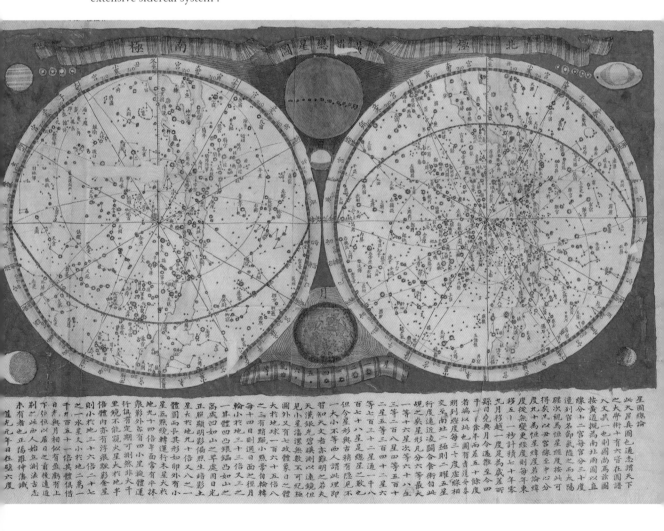

COINING THE ASTEROID

The list of William Herschel's discoveries, aided by his sister Caroline, continued to expand. Via the unequalled power of his telescope he also found the two moons of Saturn – Mimas and Enceladus; and the two largest moons of Uranus – Titania and Oberon. (All were given their names after Herschel's death by his son John.) He also measured the axial tilt of Mars, and made the discovery that the Martian ice caps first observed by Giovanni Domenico Cassini (1625–1712) in 1666, and Christiaan Huygens (1629–1695) in 1672, varied in size with the planet's seasons. Through his own experiments separating light with a prism, Herschel measured the temperatures of the different colours. This led to a most surprising discovery – that the highest temperature of all was recorded just *beyond* the red portion of the spectrum where there appeared to be no colour at all – this would be known as 'infrared' radiation, vital for the spectroscopic science.

The astronomer Giuseppe Piazzi.

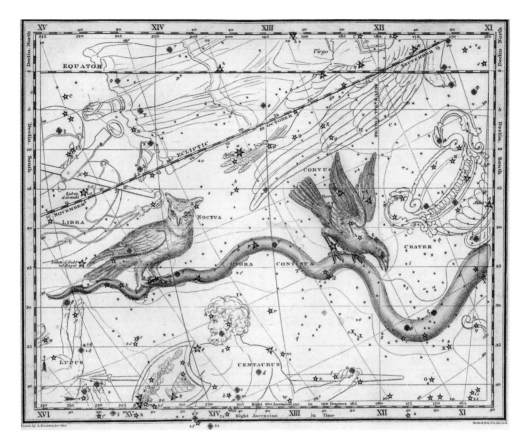

While Herschel's status as Europe's foremost manufacturer of powerful observational equipment was unsurpassed, the science of instrument-making continued apace. In London, the mathematician and virtuoso inventor Jesse Ramsden (1735–1800) produced one of the first advanced 'dividing engines', a device that allowed makers to mark ultra-fine graduations (measuring scales) on instruments, improving the accuracy with which they could be used to record. A particularly creative triumph of Ramsden's workshop and its dividing engine emerged in 1789: a unique upright wheel, which featured two opposite-facing scopes at its centre to measure altitude. The instrument was a special commission for the astronomical observatory at Palermo, Sicily, the most southern of Europe's observatories; and, on its arrival, the Italian Catholic priest Giuseppe Piazzi (1746–1826) embarked on creating his own star catalogue.

As the nineteenth century opened, Piazzi using the 'Palermo Circle' had marked some 8000 stars with greater accuracy than had been previously achieved; but on 1 January 1801 he noticed something unusual. A star he had catalogued

Alexander Jamieson's 1822 now obsolete constellation Noctua, in the shape of an owl. From his A Celestial Atlas (1822), of constellation maps of stars visible only to the naked eye.

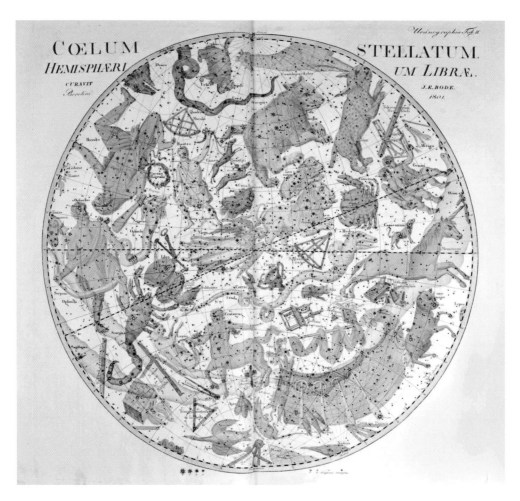

the previous night had shifted position. He checked again the following nights, and confirmed its movement and realized he'd found a new body within the solar system, perhaps even a new planet. It certainly fitted with the prediction of 'Bode's law', a hypothesis that celestial bodies orbit in a planetary sequence, suggested by Johann Elert Bode in the previous century. It was rooted in Johannes Kepler's concern with the disproportionate gap between Mars and Jupiter – surely, there had to be an undiscovered planet lying there, a hidden part of God's otherwise perfect geometry. Herschel's discovery of Uranus had worked within the predictive arrangement of Bode's law – it being the next planet beyond Saturn found within the expected ratio – and so it was thought that Piazzi's discovery, which he named Cerere Ferdinandea after the Roman goddess of agriculture and King Ferdinand of Sicily, might be that elusive Mars–Jupiter intermediary.

1801 – Uranographia *by Johann Elert Bode, 1801, the first to attempt a complete representation of all 15,000 naked-eye stars and one of the last great celestial atlases to display the skills of the astronomer–artist.*

Opposite: *The constellation* Virgo, *from* Urania's Mirror.

For half a century, this body, known as Ceres, was listed as a planet in astronomy texts. But William Herschel found it to be so small as to be almost indistinguishable in shape, apparently much smaller than Earth's Moon. When on 28 March 1802 Heinrich Olbers sighted a similarly small moving body – a 'planet' named Pallas – Herschel again found it to be of diminutive proportions. He suggested instead a new term to apply: asteroid, meaning star-like (from the Greek *asteroeides* – aster 'star' and *-eidos* 'form, shape').

In a last-ditch attempt to save the beautifully simple Bode's law, Olbers suggested that Ceres and Palas might be fragments of a long-ago destroyed planet that once filled the Mars–Jupiter gap. At first the discovery of other similarly small bodies certainly fuelled the popularity of this ghost planet theory, but as more asteroids were found (by the 1850s 'asteroid' had become a standard term for minor planets) it became clear in the late nineteenth century that, even if the bodies had indeed once been parts of the larger mass, it would have been very much smaller than Earth's Moon, and certainly not a planet.

ABOVE: *The cover of* Urania's Mirror *(1824), a collection of astronomical charts based on Alexander Jamieson's work.*

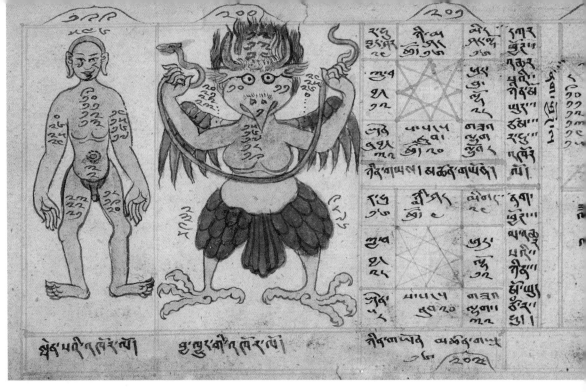

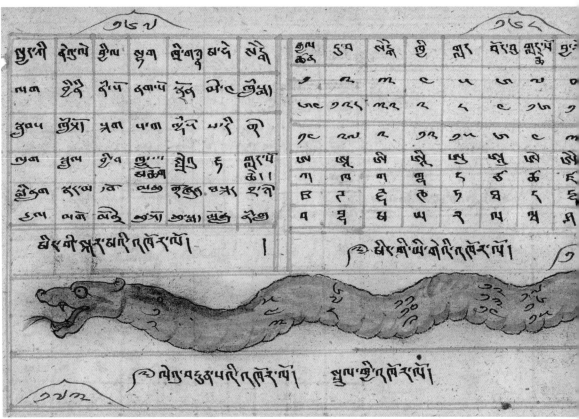

Top: *Instructions on interpreting eclipses and the zodiac.*

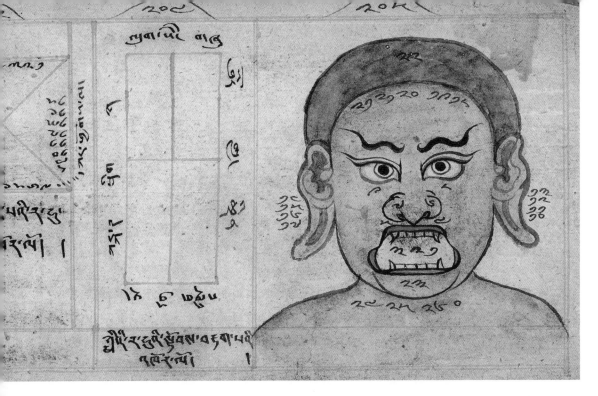

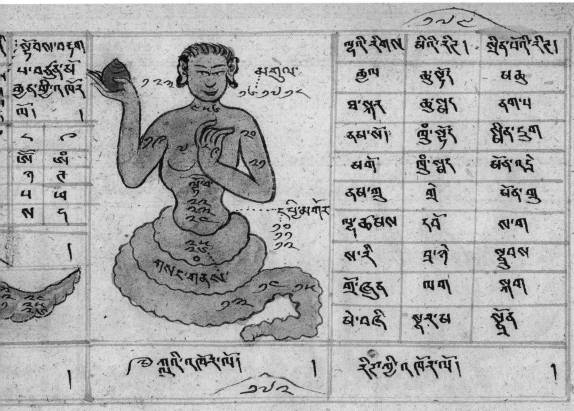

ABOVE: The naga, a mythical creature that originates in Hinduism but is often mentioned in Buddhist literature.

JOHN HERSCHEL AND THE GREAT MOON HOAX

Portrait of a man-bat, from Découvertes dans la lune…, *1836.*

On 25 August 1835, readers of the New York penny newspaper *The Sun* were stunned to read of new astronomical discoveries made by John Herschel (1792–1871), son of William and a famous astronomer in his own right. The younger Herschel had left London in November 1833 for Cape Town, where he had built a 21ft (6.4m) telescope to study the southern skies and to observe the return of Halley's Comet. *The Sun*, however, quoted Herschel's assistant Dr Andrew Grant in their report of a most remarkable discovery occurring when Herschel had turned his powerful lens towards the Moon. 'He has obtained a distinct view of objects in the Moon', the paper announced, '[and] has affirmatively settled the question whether this satellite be inhabited, and by what order of things.'

Entered according to Act of Congress, 1835 by Benj. H. Day in the Office of the Clerk of District Ct of the United States for the Southern District of New York.

LUNAR ANIMALS
AND OTHER
OBJECTS,
Discovered by Sir John Herschel in his Observatory at the Cape of Good Hope and copied from sketches
in the Edinburgh Journal of Science.

for Description, See Pamphlet Published at the Sun Office.

Over six articles, a *Sun* journalist, Richard Adams Locke, perpetrated perhaps the most famous media hoax in history, revealing increasingly elaborate discoveries made by Herschel of alien life on the lunar landscape. Readers were teased initially with reports of huge basalt formations, profusely covered in a vegetation of red flowers. Then came the equally colourful wildlife: brown bison-like quadrupeds, goats 'of a bluish lead color' and a strange, spherical amphibious creature that rolled itself at speed across a pebble beach. With the third article came the news of the bipedal beaver, who carried its young in its arms and, judging from the smoke plumes from its hut, had mastered fire. The fourth article announced the existence of the Vespertilio-homo, or 'man-bat', a hominoid species that Herschel had frequently observed being deep in rational conversation. 'Some of their amusements', however, 'would but ill comport with our terrestrial notions of decorum.' The fifth article reported the existence of an abandoned temple made of sapphire; and finally the sixth report went into further detail of the man-bats, before wrapping up with the announcement that the Sun's rays had shone down

Lunar animals and other objects discovered by Sir John Herschel in his observatory at the Cape of Good Hope and copied from sketches in the Edinburgh Journal of Science, *1835.*

Other Discoveries Made on the Moon by Mr Herschel, *1836*.

The return of an imagined sightseeing tour of Herschel's lunar discoveries.

The imagined pastimes of the lunar men: hunting, and braiding each other's hair.

Herschel's lens, causing a fire that had burnt his observatory to the ground.

Herschel had indeed made such a journey to Cape Town, but the quoted amanuensis, Dr Andrew Grant, was entirely fictitious. Locke had concocted the idea with the shameless (and successful) aim of boosting the paper's circulation, while also taking a satirical swipe at the popularity for recent outlandish astronomical theories. This included the ideas of Franz von Paula Gruithuisen, a professor of astronomy at Munich University, who in 1824 had published a paper titled *Discovery of Many Distinct Traces of Lunar Inhabitants, Especially of One of Their Colossal Buildings*. Gruithuisen claimed to have sighted colour variations that suggested vegetation, as well as signs of walls, roads, fortifications and cities. More recently the Reverend Thomas Dick, known as the 'Christian Philosopher', had calculated there to be 21.9 trillion inhabitants of the solar system. The lunar population, he stated, made up 4.2 million of this number. Dick's work was massively popular, and he counted Ralph Waldo Emerson among his fans.

There had also been some magnificent suggestions as to how to signal to alien life, on the Moon and elsewhere, using giant geometric patterns drawn in Earth's surface (similar to the Nazca Lines of southern Peru). In 1820 the German mathematician Carl Friedrich Gauss suggested using trees to set out an enormous geometric proof of the Pythagorean theorem across a large area of Siberian tundra. The shape would be so large that it would be legible to lunar eyes. In 1840 the Austrian astronomer Joseph von Littrow reportedly had the same idea but with a twist, proposing a giant circular canal be dug through the Sahara desert. Fill this with kerosene, he suggested, and ignite it. Perhaps unsurprisingly, neither idea came to fruition.

Locke though was most likely playing on the historical Herschel connection with the idea of lunar life. As we have seen, William Herschel is remembered for great and admirable achievements, but towards the end of the eighteenth century he had also explored the plausible 'plurality of worlds' theory with his own search for signs of life on the Moon (see William and Caroline Herschel entry on page 176). In correspondence with a friend, he claimed to have found it. Spying the prominent rings of the moonscape (which we know now to be the craters of asteroid impact), he interpreted the formations to be grand 'Circuses' of buildings, an arrangement that made perfect sense to him, as they allowed the optimal collection of sunshine:

> For in that shape of Building one-half will have the directed light and the other half the reflected light of the Sun. Perhaps, then on the Moon every town is one very large Circus?… Should this be true ought we not to watch the erection of any new small Circus as the Lunarians may the Building of a new Town on the Earth… By reflecting a little on the subject I am almost convinced that those numberless small Circuses we see on the Moon are the works of the Lunarians and may be called their Towns…

In addition, the *Philosophical Transactions of the Royal Society* of 1795 reveal that William Herschel's belief in extra-terrestrial habitability extended to all celestial bodies, including the Sun:

> The sun… appears to be nothing else than a very eminent, large and lucid planet, evidently the first, or in strictness of speaking, the only primary one of our system… Its similarity to the other globes of the solar system… leads us to suppose that it is most probably inhabited… by beings whose organs are adapted to the peculiar circumstances of that vast globe.

John Herschel, 1867.

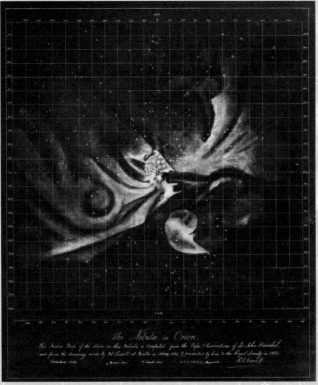

ABOVE: *The first photograph of the Moon, a daguerreotype made by John William Draper in 1840.*

LEFT: The Nebula in Orion *by Robert Stirling Newall, 1884. The engineer and astronomer based his map on the 1830s' observations of John Herschel while in South Africa.*

OPPOSITE TOP: *Whirlpool Galaxy, or Messier 51a, sketched by William Parsons, 3rd Earl of Rosse, in 1845. The first sketch of a spiral nebula (galaxy).*

OPPOSITE BOTTOM: *The Leviathan of Parsonstown, built by William Parsons, 3rd Earl of Rosse, with which he drew the architecture of nebulae and discovered the spiral structure of the Whirlpool Galaxy.*

NEPTUNE IDENTIFIED

William Herschel's discovery of Uranus in 1781 and indeed
Piazzi's finding of Ceres had been happy accidents, anomalies
discernible by their unexpected movement. Neptune, on the
other hand, demonstrates the astronomical progress that had
been made by the mid-nineteenth century, for it was the first
planet to be discovered with purely mathematical prediction,
rather than empirical observation. Just as races for glory were
increasingly common in the field of Victorian exploration
(with the searches for the Northwest Passage and, later, the
geographic poles spurring on such competition), so too was
there a scramble to find Neptune.

Too dim to be visible to the naked eye, the planet's existence
had been hypothesized since shortly after the discovery of
Uranus, when a colleague of Bode – Placidus Fixlmillner –
had incorporated its previous positions recorded by Tobias
Mayer and John Flamsteed (both thinking it to be a star)

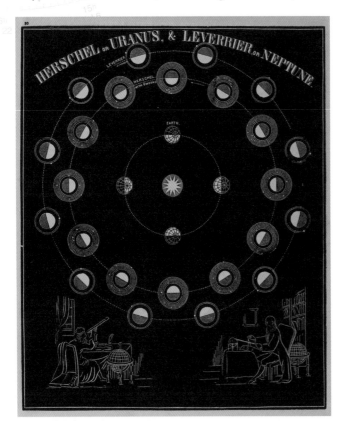

*The planetary discoveries
of William Herschel and
Urbain Le Verrier marked
in Smith's* Introduction to
Astronomy, *1850.*

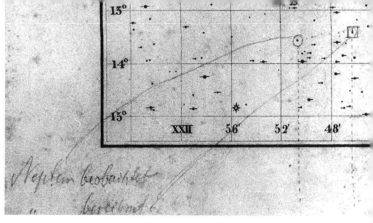

The original chart used by Le Verrier and Galle to find Neptune.

to produce a table predicting the planet's future movements. Uranus, however, soon began to deviate from this expected course, and though its forecast was refined in 1790, by the 1830s its movements were again noticeably perturbed.

Theories abounded as to why this was. Was there underestimated gravitational pull from Jupiter and Saturn? Perhaps some sort of invisible cosmic fluid obstructed its path? Or could the understanding of the inverse law of attraction at such distance need rethinking? Another possibility was that there was an undiscovered planet influencing its movements with its own gravity. In November 1845, the French astronomer Urbain Le Verrier (1811–1877) delivered an investigation of this last idea to the Paris Academy of Sciences. Drawing on Bode's law, Le Verrier guessed that the next planet in the successive arrangement lay beyond Uranus with a longitude (at that time) from the Sun at around 325 degrees.

Earlier in Cambridge in October 1843, a young student named John Couch Adams (1819–1892) had come to a similar conclusion, and in September 1845 offered a specific (and similar) prediction of 323 degrees 34 minutes. The two were unaware of the proximity of their guesses until the following year, when Le Verrier's paper reached Cambridge.

The race was on to find the purported planet in the specified neighbourhood via high-powered telescope, and to compare the sky with the latest star charts to locate any inexplicable changes. Adams's chances of primacy lay in the hands of James Challis (1803–1882), professor of astronomy at Cambridge, who lacked up-to-date maps. Le Verrier, meanwhile, had called on the help of the Berlin Observatory, which had access to the Berlin Academy's new Star Atlas, unpublished in the United Kingdom. The search began, and ended, on 23 September 1846 when a star was found in the sky by Johann Galle (1812–1910) that was not on the map, within a degree of Le Verrier's prediction. Neptune, the fourth-largest planet by diameter in the solar system, had been found. (Le Verrier modestly proposed naming the planet Le Verrier, but outside France this idea was fiercely opposed, and by the end of the year Neptune had become the internationally accepted name.)

THE PHANTOM PLANET: VULCAN

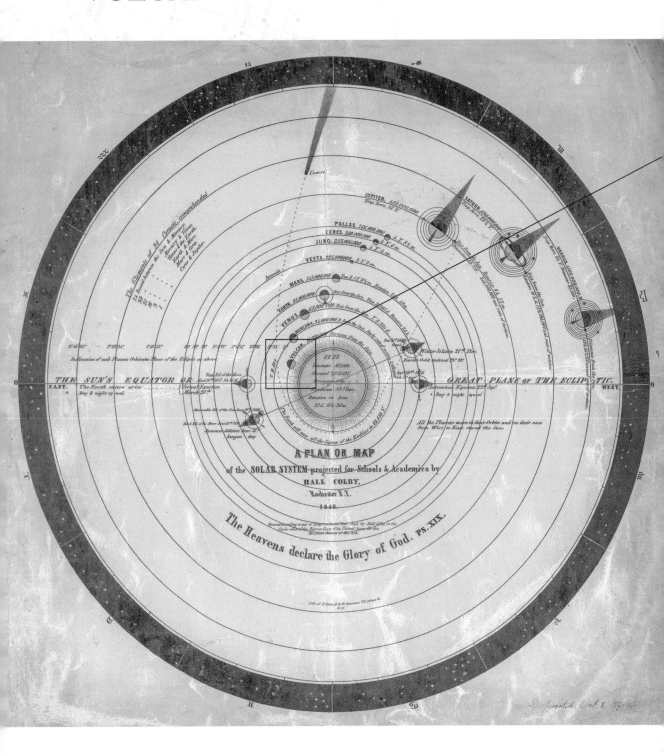

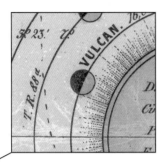

Triumphant with his discovery of Neptune, Urbain Le Verrier turned his attention to a puzzle first handed to him in 1840 by François Arago, the director of the Paris Observatory – Mercury's orbital motion around the Sun. Having devised a predictive model for the planet's course, the astronomer had been perplexed to find, in 1843, that his figures did not match observations. He threw himself into the challenge and, in 1859, published a considerably more careful study, yet still found there to be an inexplicable discrepancy. For some mysterious reason, Mercury's 'perihelion' (the point where a celestial body comes closest to the Sun) was advancing slightly faster than expected – a phenomenon called perihelion precession. Specifically it was off by the amount of 43 arcseconds (a sixtieth of a minute of angular distance) per century; such a relatively minuscule variation illustrates just how advanced celestial mechanics with its Newtonian basis had advanced by this time. Le Verrier announced that the most likely explanation was the existence of an undiscovered planet in orbit between the Sun and Mercury, and of about the same size as the latter. Given its proximity to the Sun, this new planet should naturally be called Vulcan after the Roman god of fire and volcanoes.

Given Le Verrier's previous success, there was little reason to find fault in his claims, but he still needed empirical observations to solidify the theory. This appeared to come surprisingly quickly. In that same year of 1859 he was contacted by a French physician and amateur astronomer named Edmond Modeste Lescarbault, from the town of Orgères-en-Beauce, who was certain he had observed just such a planet via his humble 3.75in (95mm) refractor, passing before the Sun earlier that year. Le Verrier rushed to visit Lescarbault. Satisfied with the doctor's skill and his measurement of the transit of one hour, seventeen minutes and nine seconds, he announced Vulcan's existence at a meeting of the Académie des sciences in Paris. The planet, he said, revolved around the Sun at a distance of 13 million miles (21 million km), for a period of nineteen days and seven hours.

OPPOSITE AND INSET: A Plan or Map of the Solar System Projected for Schools & Academies *(1846), charting the non-existent planet Vulcan, nearest the Sun, at a distance of 16 million miles (26 million km). The asteroids Vesta, Juno, Ceres and Pallas are also marked.*

Le Verrier soon started receiving a number of reports supporting his assertion, though none could be verified. In January 1860, four observers in London claimed to have seen an alleged transit in 1860; in March 1862, a Mr Lummis of Manchester, England, swore to have made a similar observation, and so on. In July 1878, two experienced observers – Professor James Craig Watson (director of the Ann Arbor Observatory in Michigan) and Lewis Swift (from Rochester, New York) – claimed to have seen a Vulcan-type planet, which both described as red. It later turned out, when their figures were corrected, that they had sighted known stars. Neither confirmed nor denied, the search for the elusive planet Vulcan continued into the twentieth century. Following the publication of Albert Einstein's theory of general relativity in 1916 the phantom* was finally exorcized, with the revolutionary rethinking of the gravity of classical mechanics that finally accounted for the perihelion discrepancy. This was verified with the solar eclipse of 29 May 1919, and the existence of a planet inside the orbit of Mercury was concluded to be impossible.

OPPOSITE: *Colourful 2017 composite images of the planet Mercury, using earlier findings from the* Messenger *mission.* Messenger's *discovery of fresh, cliff-like landforms led scientists to conclude that, 4.5 billion years after the solar system was formed, Mercury is still shrinking.*

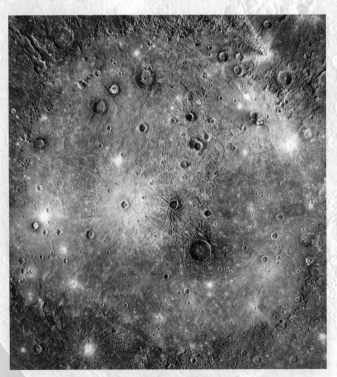

With such a thin atmosphere Mercury has little to protect itself from space debris, and so its surface is riddled with craters. This colour mosaic shows a particularly spectacular crater called the Caloris Basin, which is circled by mile-high mountains and stretches about 950 miles (1525 km) across. (For scale, the state of Texas is 773 miles (1244 km) wide.)

*For an entire collection of these kinds of ghost features on maps, see *The Phantom Atlas* (Simon and Schuster, 2016).

SPECTROSCOPY AND THE DAWN OF ASTROPHYSICS

As we approach the twentieth century, an era of tremendous acceleration in cosmic discovery, it is perhaps useful to take stock of the developmental stages reached thus far. Astronomy had, since its origins in the shapeless mists of antiquity, served the purpose of prediction, to represent the movements of the planets with a reliable model, using material concepts such as the spheres of the ancient Greeks, driven by divine power. With Kepler, the scientific causes of this force became the question for the astronomer, with the sky still a realm divorced from the physics of the terrestrial. With Newtonian science

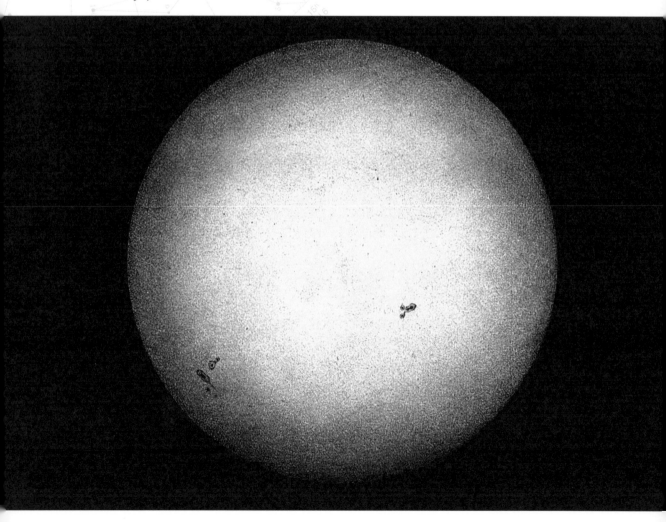

came the emergence of a unified physics, in which the same scientific laws applied to both Heaven and Earth, and though it was now suggested both were composed of the same materials the technology to prove this did not exist.

With Newton's mathematical Rosetta Stone, astronomers pursued ever more precise observation of planetary movement and star positioning into the late nineteenth century, armed with the mirrors and lenses that amplified human eyesight to a godlike factor. But as charts filled with new planets, stars and asteroids through a series of discoveries, and as mapping came to merge with the new technology of photography,* the preoccupation now was with the question of what exactly were these celestial bodies composed? A new branch of astronomy concerned with the physical nature of the heavens was required – a science of 'astrophysics'.

To investigate the celestial compositions, there was, of course, no way yet to touch the Heavens, but there was a new way to see them. The key to this was the prism. In 1666 Isaac

*A curious Victorian sky myth, specifically to do with lightning, appeared with the arrival of photography. Keraunography was the nineteenth-century belief that lightning functioned like a camera flash, and that people and animals struck by it were imprinted with a photographic image of their surroundings. The myth originated from early legends of the 1300s to 1600s, in which people struck by lightning in churches were said to have been etched with crosses; and from the fact that lightning burns do take patterned forms. The myth is hinted at by the modern term 'keraunographic marks', which are also known as 'lightning flowers'.

OPPOSITE: *The first detailed photographs of the Sun's surface were taken through a telescope in 1845, by the French physicists Jean Foucault and Armand-Hippolyte-Louis Fizeau. This allowed the confirmation of the work of Heinrich Schwabe two years earlier, who after seventeen years of observations identified a cycle in solar sunspot numbers, providing the first clue to the internal composition of the Sun.*

From the catalogue of solar and stellar spectra by the Jesuit Angelo Secchi, c.1870.

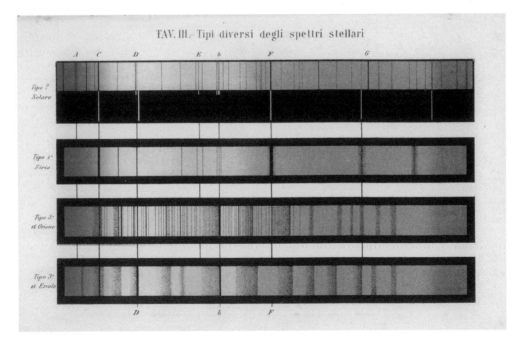

TAV. III.—Tipi diversi degli spettri stellari

A solar corona at eclipse photographed by a Harvard College expedition at Shelbyville, Kentucky, 7 August 1869.

Newton had bought a triangular glass prism 'to try therewith the celebrated Phaenomena of Colours'. He directed a shaft of sunlight through a prism and projected its constituent rainbow colours onto a screen. The prevailing belief at that time was that all coloured light was white light that had somehow been transformed. Newton showed that, in fact, white light had a compound nature, possessing a 'spectrum' (Latin for

An early photograph of a total solar eclipse, printed in 1862.

apparition), and proved this to be the case by using a lens to recombine the colours to form white light.

In a similar experiment performed later by the British chemist William Hyde Wollaston (1766–1828), it was noticed that there were fine lines between the colours, appearing to border each band. The Bavarian lens manufacturer Joseph Fraunhofer (1787–1826), who examined with a telescope (the first basic spectroscope) the spectrum produced by his own prism found there to be hundreds of these dark brown lines, today known as Fraunhofer lines, in the spectrum. A notable breakthrough was made by Robert Bunsen (1811–1899) and Gustav Kirchhoff (1824–1887), who put chemical compounds into a flame (the famed Bunsen Burner) and discovered that specific lines among light corresponded to particular chemical elements. Light, it transpired, was a message from the stars, a broadcast of their composition.

By matching specific lines with metals, Bunsen and Kirchhoff were able to find two new elements using this celestial information, naming them after their spectral line: caesium (from the Latin for blue-grey) and rubidium (red). Applying this technique meant that several metals were identified as existing in the Sun – a discovery of composition that had always been considered unknowable.

Bunsen and Kirchhoff's method swiftly became key practice in chemistry. In 1862 the Swedish physicist Anders Jonas Ångström (1814–1874) combined spectroscopy and photography to prove that the Sun's atmosphere contained hydrogen, among other elements, and by the 1880s more than fifty elements had been identified in the spectrum of the Sun – a tremendous advancement in solar physics. The discovery had not come without difficulty, however. Bunsen spent years performing hundreds of spectroscopic tests on crystallized elements, measuring and recording the spectra they emitted. Finally, in May 1874, he completed his giant manuscript of results, and went to lunch to celebrate. He returned a few hours later and found his work reduced to ashes. A flask of water on his desk had, ironically, concentrated the Sun's rays and incinerated his papers. He wrote of his despair in letters to friends, and then began the work again.

There also began an investigation into the nature of the surface of the Sun. In laboratories, the white light spectrum was successfully recreated using solids or liquid metals under

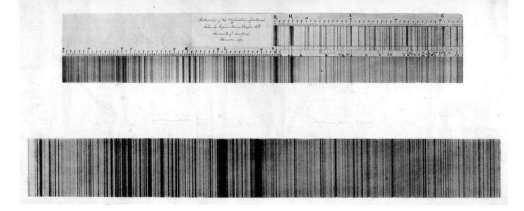

extremely high temperatures, which suggested that the Sun's surface was, at the very least, a hot liquid if not a burning ball of metal. The search for answers was aided in the second half of the nineteenth century by a series of solar eclipses, when the Moon passed before the Sun obscuring its body from view. These allowed the study of the solar atmosphere from specially built observatories around Europe. Gradually through these observations an idea of the layers of the Sun's atmosphere was formed. As the Sun's gaseous outer layers under high pressure discharged a white light spectrum, it was realized that perhaps all light emitted was produced by gas.

The American astronomer Henry Draper (1837–1882) took the first photograph of the spectrum of a star, Vega, in 1872, showing absorption lines that revealed its chemical makeup. Astronomers began to see that spectroscopy was the key to understanding how stars evolve. Following his death in 1882, Draper's work led to the publication of the Henry Draper Catalogue *between 1918 and 1924, which gave spectroscopic classifications for 225,300 stars.*

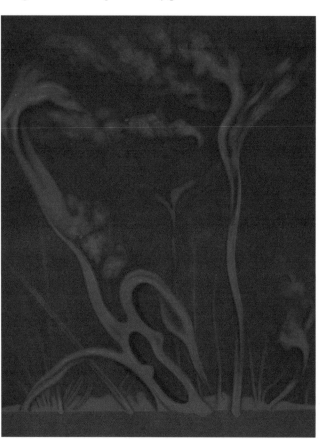

A depiction of solar prominences by the French astronomer Étienne Léopold Trouvelot (1827–1895), one of the great scientific artists.

The English astronomer Norman Lockyer, who had earlier coined the term 'chromosphere' for a layer surrounding the Sun, and the French physicist Pierre Janssen were both struck independently by the same brainwave – that solar prominences (the large visible protruding eruptions that can last from a day to months)

could be viewed and analyzed at any time of year by using a spectroscope that greatly dispersed the spectrum. No longer was it necessary to rely on solar eclipses for viewing. One direct result of this was the confirmation by Janssen and, separately, Lockyer, that an unknown yellow spectral line signature was an entirely new element. Lockyer named it helium, after Helios, the Greek Titan of the Sun.

While others studied the Sun, on 29 August 1864 William Huggins (1824–1910) – one of the fathers of astrophysics – became the first to measure the spectrum of a planetary nebula. He was also the first to distinguish between nebulae and galaxies through the characteristics of their spectra.

A plaster model of a 'normal lunar crater', the cause of which, argue James Nasmyth and James Carpenter in their book The Moon *(1874), was volcanic activity – a popular Victorian notion that was only put to rest by lunar exploration following the Moon landing of 1969.*

CELESTIAL PHENOMENA: PART TWO

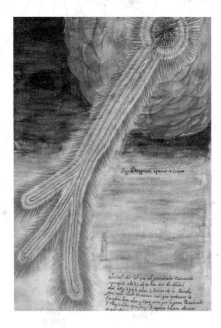

ABOVE: *The meteorite seen over the skies of Terrassa, Catalonia, in 1704.*

BELOW: *The Leonid meteor storm shower in 1833, from the* Bilderatlas der Sternenwelt *by Edward Weiss.*

ABOVE: *Amédée Guillemin's illustration of Donati's Comet, first observed on 2 June 1858. Image taken from* Les comètes *(1875).*

BELOW: *A chart of the spectacular meteor shower observed over London on 13 November 1866.*

ABOVE: Passing events… *by George Cruikshank, a densely detailed satire in comet form of the year 1853 (which included observations of four separate comets).*

RIGHT: *Shooting stars from Rambosson's* Astronomy, *1875.*

BELOW: *Detail from Rambosson's* Astronomy, *1875.*

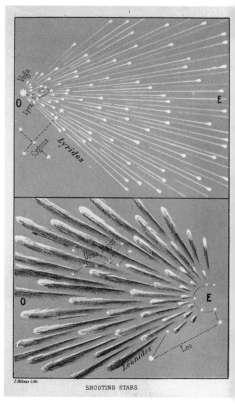

SHOOTING STARS

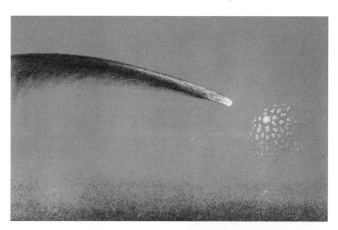

Maria Mitchell.

LEFT: *In 1847 American astronomer Maria Mitchell (1818–1889) discovered a comet today classified as C/1847 T1, and known as 'Miss Mitchell's Comet'. She was awarded a gold medal by King Frederick VI of Denmark in 1848 and enjoyed worldwide fame.*

(See also Celestial Phenomena: Part One on page 112.)

PERCIVAL LOWELL SPIES LIFE ON MARS

'MARS INHABITED' cried the headline of the *New York Times* on 30 August 1907, citing the claims of Percival Lowell (1855–1916), founder of the Lowell Observatory, Flagstaff, Arizona, following the recent 'opposition' (the term for when Earth and Mars pass relatively close by in their orbits of the

Maps of four aspects of the surface of Mars, drawn by Giovanni Schiaparelli in September 1877, when the planet was close to Earth.

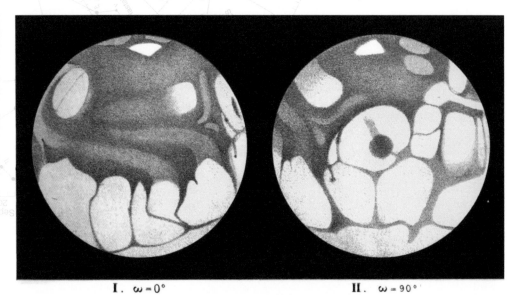

I. ω = 0°   II. ω = 90°

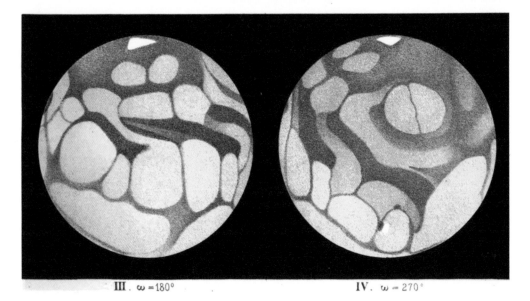

III. ω = 180°   IV. ω = 270°

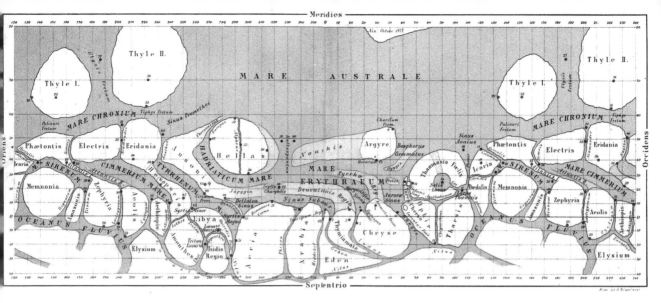

Schiaparelli's map of the planet Mars, from its southern pole to the fortieth parallel, and its 'canals'. Based on his 1877–1878 observations.

Sun) that had provided easier observation of the red planet's surface. 'After the melting of the south polar cap had got well under way', said Lowell, 'canals began to make their appearance about it. It is a direct sequitur from this that the planet is at present the abode of intelligent constructive life… my observations since have fully confirmed it. No other supposition is consonant with all the facts here.' The problem, though, was not just with the supposition, but also the facts.

Lowell observing Venus from the observer's chair of the 24in (60cm) refracting telescope at the Lowell Observatory, 1896.

FOLLOWING PAGES: A map of Mars and its channels, from Sir William Peck's A Popular Handbook and Atlas of Astronomy… (1891).

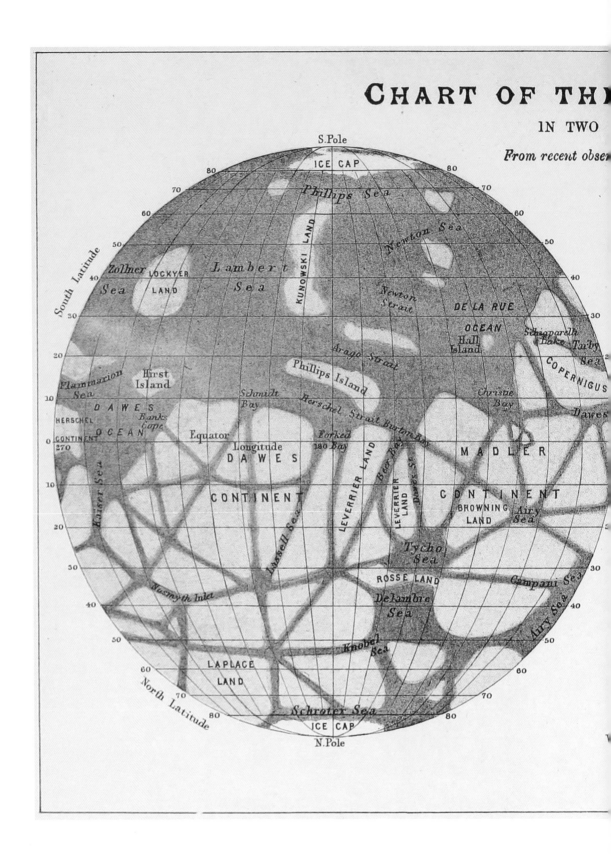

CHART OF TH[E]

IN TWO

From recent obser[vations]

S.Pole

ICE CAP

80   80

70   70

Phillips Sea

60   60

Newton Sea

50   50

South Latitude

Zöllner   LOCKYER   *Lambert*   KUNOWSKI LAND   *Newton*   DE LA RUE
40   *Sea*   LAND   *Sea*   *Strait*   40

Sea   OCEAN
30   *Hall*   *Schiaparelli*   30
Island   *Lake* *Tarby*
Sea

20   *Arago Strait*   COPERNIGUS   20

Flammarion   *Hirst*   *Phillips Island*   *Christie*   *Dawes*
Sea   *Island*   *Bay*
10   *Schmidt*   *Herschel Strait* *Burton Bay*   10
DAWES   *Bay*
HERSCHEL   *Banks*
CONTINENT   OCEAN   *Cape*   *Forked*   MADLER
0   *Equator*   *120 Bay*   0
270   *Longitude*
DAWES   LEVERRIER LAND   LEVERRIER LAND   CONTINENT
10   *Bear Bay*   10
CONTINENT   BROWNING   *Airy*
LAND   *Sea*
20   20
Tycho
Sea
30   ROSSE LAND   *Campani Sea*   30
Nasmyth Inlet   *Lassell Sea*   *Delambre*
Sea   *Airy Sea*
40   40
50   *Knobel*   50
LAPLACE   *Sea*
60   LAND   60
North Latitude   70   70
80   80
Schroter Sea
ICE CAP
N.Pole

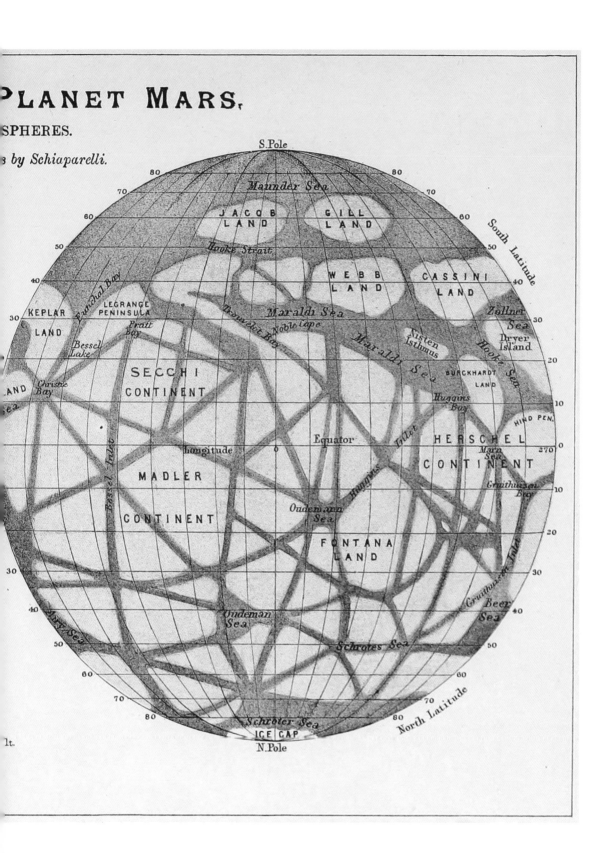

PLANET MARS,

SPHERES.

by Schiaparelli.

S.Pole

Maunder Sea

JACOB LAND   GILL LAND

Hooke Strait

WEBB LAND   CASSINI LAND

South Latitude

KEPLAR LAND   LEGRANGE PENINSULA   Maraldi Sea   Zöllner Sea

Funchal Bay   Pratt Bay   Noble Cape   Kisten Isthmus   Dreyer Island

Bessel Lake   Bramelot Bay   Maraldi Sea   Hooke Sea

Christie Bay   SECCHI CONTINENT   BURCKHARDT LAND

Huggins Bay

HIND PEN.

Equator   Inlet   HERSCHEL CONTINENT   270

Longitude   0   Marn Sea

Bessel Inlet   MADLER   Huggins   Gruithuisen Bay

CONTINENT   Oudeman Sea

FONTANA LAND

Oudeman Sea   Gruithuisen Inlet

Sea   Beer Sea

Schroter Sea

North Latitude

Schroter Sea

ICE CAP

N.Pole

lt.

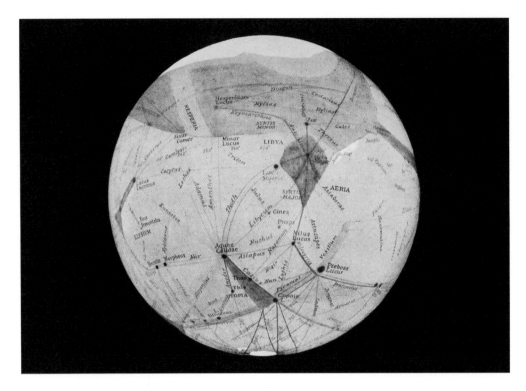

Lowell's Mars, based on his
sketched observations of Martian
canals and oases.

Lowell had abandoned the cotton trade in the late
nineteenth century to follow a passion for astronomy, choosing
Flagstaff for the site of an observatory because of its ideal
remoteness, altitude and clear skies. Inspired by the work of
the French astronomer Camille Flammarion, he became
obsessed with the observation of Mars, in particular the 'canals'
(i.e. artificially made waterways) on its surface, which were first
described by the Italian astronomer Giovanni Schiaparelli
(1835–1910) following the Great Opposition of 1877, when the
planet approached within 35 million miles (56 million km) of
Earth. Here we reach the root of the 'Martian life' confusion
that would grip Victorian imagination for more than forty years.
Schiaparelli originally labelled the dark flowing lines that he
sighted at the Martian Poles with the word canali ('channels').
This was mistranslated as 'canal', and with the implication of
deliberate construction now attached, the study of planetary
astronomy was launched on a most peculiar trajectory.

Though he was not the only sky-gazer in thrall to the canal
delusion, Lowell did more than most to popularize the notion,
spending fifteen years studying, mapping and writing on the
clear evidence of Martian life, publishing an eccentric trilogy
of reference works: *Mars* (1895), *Mars and its Canals* (1906) and

Mars as the Abode of Life (1908). The astronomical community remained sceptical. The canals were proving extraordinarily elusive to other observers, and Lowell's sightings were difficult to photographically reproduce with definition. Finally in 1909 the powerful 60in (1.5m) Mount Wilson Observatory telescope in southern California provided closer scrutiny of the dark Martian 'canals', and showed them to be irregular but naturally formed geological features, likely the result of natural erosion.

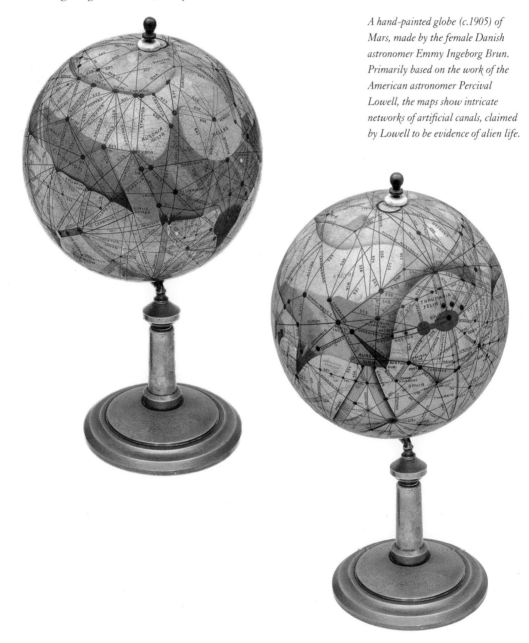

A hand-painted globe (c.1905) of Mars, made by the female Danish astronomer Emmy Ingeborg Brun. Primarily based on the work of the American astronomer Percival Lowell, the maps show intricate networks of artificial canals, claimed by Lowell to be evidence of alien life.

THE SEARCH FOR PLANET X
AND THE DISCOVERY OF PLUTO

Percival Lowell was wrong, and his theories on Martian life
were brought crashing to the ground. In his observations
of Venus, too, which he had begun in 1896, he produced
controversial – and later disproved – sightings of dark features
on the planet's pole. In 2003 a study concluded that this was

most likely due to his 'stopping down' (reducing the aperture of the lens to reduce the interference of daylight) to such an extent that he, in effect, turned his telescope into a giant ophthalmoscope – the dark features that he saw were actually shadows of the blood vessels in his own eye.

Although this has often led to Lowell being painted as a crackpot, there is much to admire about his work, particularly in his later years, which were spent in pursuit of 'Planet X' – an undiscovered ninth planet of the solar system that he was certain existed, displacing Uranus and Neptune from their predicted positions with its gravity. With the assistance of Elizabeth Langdon Williams (1879–1981), one of the earliest female graduates of the Massachusetts Institute of Technology, and a team of other human 'computers', the Lowell Observatory team performed a series of calculations to pinpoint likely locations for this theoretical new planet.

Following Lowell's death on 12 November 1916, the search continued for eleven years, after which Percival's nephew Abbott Lawrence Lowell took over the observatory and installed a new photographic instrument known as an astrograph to aid in the search. A young Kansas man named Clyde Tombaugh (1906– 1997) was given the job of scouring the skies, in the regions dictated by Percival Lowell's predictions. On 18 February 1930 Tombaugh compared photos of the sky with those made the previous month, and spotted an object that appeared to have jumped positions. Under further observation, it became clear the object had an orbit beyond that of Neptune, ruling out the possibility of it being an asteroid. Tombaugh had found a new planet (later to be officially downgraded to a dwarf planet in 2006), apparently the X for which Lowell had so desperately searched.* An eleven-year-old English schoolgirl, Venetia Burney, suggested the name of Pluto after the Roman god of the Underworld.

After his death in 1997 at the age of ninety, Clyde Tombaugh fittingly embarked on his own posthumous journey. A portion of his ashes was placed aboard the *New Horizons* interplanetary spacecraft, which in 2015 performed the first flyby of Pluto, passing just 7800 miles (12,500km) above its surface.

OPPOSITE: *An enhanced multispectral colour view of Pluto captured by the National Aeronautics and Space Administration's (NASA) New Horizons spacecraft on 14 July 2015. The many colours represent a complex geology and climate that we are only just beginning to decode. The spacecraft's discovery of icy mountains 11,000ft (3350m) high suggest a mysterious source of geological activity.*

*There is mounting evidence that a real, and enormous, Planet X, referred to as Planet Nine by modern astronomers, may be lurking far beyond Neptune, awaiting discovery in the next few decades. This would, for example, explain the strange movements of some objects in the Kuiper Belt – a collection of bodies in the outer solar system.

ORGANIZING THE STARS: 'PICKERING'S WOMEN'

The most famous of the turn-of-the-century rooms of 'human computers' was to be found at Harvard University, where a team of skilled female calculators and data gatherers was assembled by the university's director, Edward C. Pickering (1846–1919) following the death of the astronomer and pioneering astrophotographer Henry Draper in 1882. 'Pickering's women', as they were nicknamed, were to take on the enormous challenge of continuing Draper's work, building a new catalogue of stellar classification.

Since antiquity, stars had been categorized by their brightness in orders of magnitude – an ultimately subjective estimation, with the first order being the brightest, the sixth the faintest. The arrival of the telescope had brought many more stars into view that previously were too faint to be visible, and so the orders of magnitude were increased in rank to accommodate

The 'Observatory Group' of Harvard computers, c.1910.

A group of the Harvard
computers at work, 1891.

the busying star fields, which, of course, afforded greater disparity in subjective classification. In 1856 the English astronomer Norman Pogson (1829–1891) followed through on a realization that had struck Edmond Halley a century before – that stars of the first order of magnitude were 100 times brighter than those of the sixth order, and so from this a specific scale of measurement could be ascertained. Add to this the improvements in astrophotography, incorporating the stellar colour spectrum (it was realized, for example, that hotter stars emitted a greater amount of blue light), and a much more accurate technique for magnitude measurement was available at the end of the nineteenth century. Now it needed to be applied to the skies of stars, of both new and old discovery. Pickering tasked the Harvard women with recording the brightness, position and colours of the stars, as part of the grand mission to conduct a spectroscopic study of both northern and southern skies. The group, which included Williamina Fleming, Henrietta Swan Leavitt, Florence Cushman, Anna Winlock and Antonia Maury (niece of

Annie Jump Cannon, one of 'Pickering's women', in 1922.

Henry Draper), compared modern photography with existing catalogues, allowing for distortive factors such as atmospheric refraction, often working for free to gain experience.

Notable among these extraordinary women was Annie Jump Cannon (1863–1941), who displayed a particular talent that she quickly fashioned into a formidable skill – 'Miss Cannon is the only person in the world – man or woman – who can do this work so quickly', declared Pickering of his dazzling assistant. The achievements of Cannon are staggering. She manually classified more stars in a lifetime than any other astronomer in history, amassing a total of c.350,000 stars. Her discoveries included 300 variable stars, five novae and one spectroscopic binary – the last being systems in which stars are so close together that even with a telescope they appear to be one, and so difficult to identify – and she built a bibliography of c.200,000 references. Her rate of star cataloguing grew remarkably: in her first three years she had classified 1000 stars;

by 1913 she was processing 200 stars per hour. This she did by glancing at their spectral patterns and, with a magnifying glass, classifying their brightness down to the ninth magnitude, which is about sixteen times fainter than the human eye can detect. She categorized stars with her own system of spectral classes 'O, B, A, F, G, K, M' – astronomy students use the mnemonic 'Oh Be A Fine Girl, Kiss Me' to recall her stellar classification. Through all this, she maintained a high degree of accuracy. On 9 May 1922 the International Astronomical Union passed a resolution to formally adopt Cannon's stellar classification system. It continues to be used for classification today.

The British-American astrophysicist Cecilia Payne-Gaposchkin (1900–1979), who upturned conventional thinking in 1925 with her doctoral thesis that the constitution of stars was directly linked to the abundance of hydrogen and helium in the universe. At the time it was thought that there were no noteworthy differences between the elemental composition of the Sun and Earth.

NEW VISIONS OF THE UNIVERSE:
EINSTEIN, LEMAÎTRE AND HUBBLE

The Barritt-Serviss Star and Planet Finder (1906), a tool for the amateur astronomer.

While Annie Jump Canon and her Harvard colleagues were charting the stars, and as Percival Lowell hunted for his Martians, an assistant examiner at the Swiss Federal Office for Intellectual Property in Bern was developing ideas that would form, in the words of the Russian physicist Lev Landau, 'the most beautiful of theories'. In 1905, Albert Einstein (1879–1955) published his first theory of relativity (referred to today as 'special relativity')

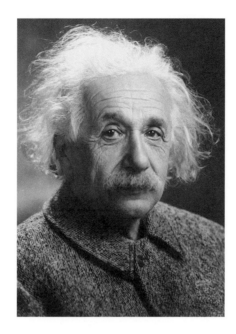

Albert Einstein.

in the journal *Annalen der Physik* ('Annals of Physics'), which explains how to interpret motion between different inertial frames of reference – that is, places that are moving at constant speeds relative to each other. The theory was based on two key principles: the principle of relativity, that the laws of physics don't change, even for objects moving at constant speed; and the principle of the speed of light, a speed that is the same for all observers, regardless of their motion in relation to the light source. (This speed is written using the symbol 'c'.) The infamous equation, $E = mc^2$, expressed the fact that mass and energy are the same physical entity, and can be changed into each other. Put simply, the increased relativistic mass (m) of a body times the speed of light squared (c^2) is equal to the kinetic energy (E) of that body.

While working at the patent office, Einstein then had his 'happiest thought' – that his principle of relativity could be extended to gravitational fields, radically revising the accepted Newtonian understanding. Two centuries earlier, Isaac Newton had pictured his 'force of gravity' as a force somehow exerted between objects, despite there apparently being nothing between them. The planets moved through this empty space of the universe on a true course, until their trajectories were curved by the effect of this force. How this force worked, however, was a question that Newton didn't even pretend to answer.

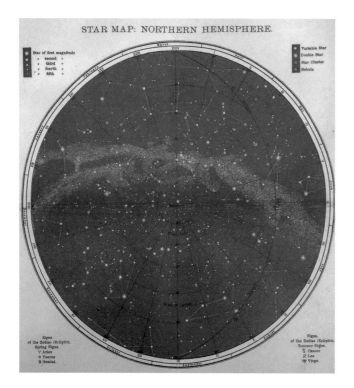

STAR MAP: NORTHERN HEMISPHERE.

A star map of the celestial northern hemisphere published in 1905, the same year that Einstein published his first theory of relativity.

As an influence on his own ideas of gravity, Einstein had at his disposal the pioneering work of British scientists Michael Faraday (1791–1867) and James Clark Maxwell (1831–1879), who for the first time brought together electricity, magnetism and light as manifestations of the same phenomenon – the electromagnetic field. To Einstein, the son of an electrical engineer, it seemed that gravity worked in the same manner, with a gravitational field, which he set about resolving with equations. His genius was in imagining where this field could be found – not as a diffuse entity that filled space like the electromagnetic field, but as *space itself*. This is the essence of his general theory of relativity, which he published in 1915.

One way to understand the idea is with the analogous image of a person lying on a trampoline, with their mass causing the fabric to dip. Rolling a marble around the rim of this fabric would result in the marble spinning around this body in a spiral, its path guided not by some unseen force tugging on it, but by the slope in the fabric created by the object at the centre. Space, according to Einstein's theory, is not separate from matter but rather is a material itself, an entity that is bent, flexed and curved by the mass of celestial bodies, explaining everything from why objects fall to the ground to the planetary

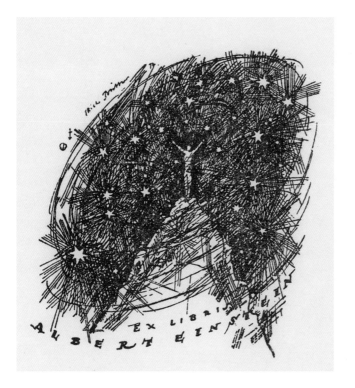

A custom bookplate designed for Albert Einstein by the painter Erich Büttner in 1917.

motions. Our massive Sun warps the space around it, causing Earth to hurtle around it like the marble rolling around the inclined wall of trampoline fabric. Einstein summarized the idea in a set of field equations, but essentially the idea in summary is this: space-time curves where there is matter. An idea beautiful in its simplicity.

From this elegant notion came bizarre predictions that have since been found to be true: for example, that light is similarly affected by gravity – as space curves around a star, its light is also deviated. In 1919 Einstein's prediction that the Sun caused such a deviation was confirmed at the Greenwich Observatory, and the effect measured. Astronomers have since exploited this phenomenon to great use. It allows us, for example, to peer around distant, massive objects like black holes to glimpse the galaxies behind them – a technique known as gravitational lensing (see Breakthroughs of the Twentieth Century, and Beyond entry on page 237 for a photograph taken by the Hubble Space Telescope exploiting this phenomenon with the galaxy cluster Abell 1689). Einstein also declared that time, too, could be curved by gravity. For example, if one twin were to live at the top of a mountain, subject to a weaker gravitational effect, with the other at the base of a valley, time would pass

Sunday,
December 14, 1919

The New York Times

Rotogravure
Picture Section, 5
In Two Parts

LATEST AND MOST REMARKABLE PHOTOGRAPH OF THE SUN

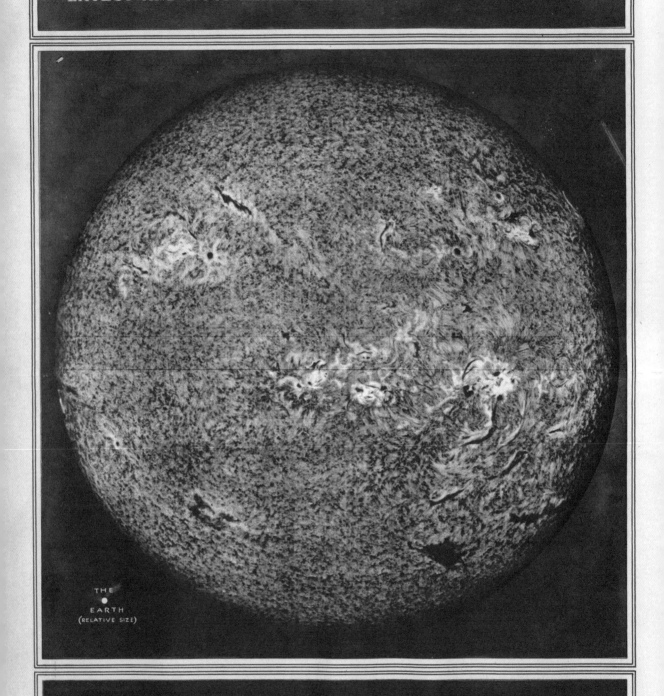

THE
EARTH
(RELATIVE SIZE)

THIS PICTURE WAS TAKEN WITH THE SPECTROHELIOGRAPH OF THE MOUNT WILSON TOWER TELESCOPE, MOUNT WILSON OBSERVATORY, CARNEGIE INSTITUTION OF WASHINGTON, USING THE RED LIGHT OF HYDROGEN, WITH EVERY PERFECTED METHOD INTRODUCED SINCE THE FIRST PHOTOGRAPH OF THE KIND WAS OBTAINED ON MOUNT WILSON IN 1908.

The sun is here shown as it would appear to an eye capable of seeing only the red light of hydrogen, revealing the solar atmosphere thousands of miles deep, with its whirling storms, resembling tornadoes on the earth, but of colossal size, centring in sun spots. This atmosphere is perfectly transparent to ordinary vision. The large, dark objects, irregular in shape, are prominences, some of which occasionally attain heights of 200,000 miles or more. The diameter of the earth on the same scale, as shown in the lower left corner of this reproduction, would be thirteen-hundredths of an inch.

This photograph, with the sun's present spots clearly defined, draws added interest just now from the evidently groundless but apparently serious alarm which has swept over parts of the country over predictions, attributed to Professor Albert Porta of the University of Michigan, that the earth may be visited between Wednesday and Friday of this week with the worst electric and weather catastrophe in history, due to an expected sun spot of unprecedented size, caused by the combined "electro-magnetic pull" of the six planets, Mercury, Venus, Mars, Jupiter, Saturn, and Neptune, which will be ranged about that time on the same side of the sun. "Interesting, if true," has been, in effect, the comment of leading astronomers of the country, who have discussed the prophecy, though admitting that the relative positions, on next Wednesday, of the planets named will be as stated. The sun's diameter is 860,000 miles.

by faster for the mountaineer – an effect that has since been proven. In fact the satellite navigation systems of modern cars are designed to accommodate the fact that, for satellites, time ticks by at a faster rate than it does on the ground.

By reinventing gravity as a geometric property of space and time, or 'space-time', the theory brought in new explanations for the behaviour of objects and a revamped basis for all of physics. It painted a thrilling picture: an exploding universe composed of a rippling fabric, filled with bottomless black holes, light curvature and temporal fluctuation. While physicists busied with the myriad inquisitional doorways that this opened up, the next notable breakthrough in astronomy came not with the theoretical workings of the universe, but with its extent.

In the early twentieth century, the prevailing theory in physical cosmology was that the Milky Way was the entirety of the universe. It was a point of increasing contention, though, and the argument entered the public forum on 26 April 1920 at the American Smithsonian Museum of Natural History when the astronomers Harlow Shapley and Heber Curtis held what became known as the Great Debate on the scale of the universe. Shapley held that distant nebulae were small and within the outskirts of our own galaxy, while Curtis believed that nebulae were separate galaxies, great in both size and distance.

Opposite: 'Latest and most remarkable photograph of the Sun... taken with the spectroheliograph of the Mount Wilson tower telescope,' New York Times, *14 December 1919.*

The giant 100in (2.5m) telescope Mount Wilson Observatory, California.

In 1923 Edwin Hubble (1889–1953), an astronomer at the Mount Wilson Observatory (the location of a 100in/2.5m Hooker telescope, the largest reflector in the world at that time), embarked on a search for novae in the Andromeda nebula. This had come under increasing scrutiny since 1912, when V. M. Slipher at the Lowell Observatory had reported it nearing Earth at a velocity of 671,081mph (1,080,000km/h),

A photograph of the Andromeda nebula (galaxy), c.1900.

an unparalleled speed of any object in the universe. To Slipher this suggested that our galaxy was 'a great spiral nebula which we see from within', moving with other spiral nebulae such as Andromeda. Hubble soon found his nova in Andromeda, but as he worked his way through the years of photographic plates of the nebula taken at Mount Wilson since 1909, he realized that this wasn't a new finding, but a Cepheid variable. The star could be found on more than sixty of the plates, varying in luminosity between the eighteenth and nineteenth orders of magnitude. This was a tremendously exciting discovery, because of how Cepheid variable stars can be used to measure distance. In the 'cosmic distance ladder' (the chain of methods by which astronomers determine the distances to celestial objects), Cepheid variables are classified as 'standard candles' – objects that have a known brightness. By comparing this known period of luminosity to an object's observed brightness, the distance to the object can be calculated using the inverse-square law. This relationship between the period and luminosity for classical Cepheids was discovered by Henrietta Swan Leavitt, one of the aforementioned 'Harvard computers' (see Organizing the Stars: 'Pickering's Women' entry on page 218) in 1908, while investigating thousands of variable stars in the Magellanic Clouds. Using this, Edwin Hubble was able to determine that Earth's distance from the Andromeda nebula was more than 900,000 light years, far farther than imagined, and putting it far beyond our galaxy. (Though Hubble is often solely credited with this discovery, the Estonian astronomer Ernst Öpik had published a paper the year before in which he estimated the distance to Andromeda, using observations of its radial velocity, with greater accuracy than Hubble.) Soon Hubble had discovered twelve more Cepheids and other novae within it, and the implication became clear – the Milky Way was not the only 'island universe'. Andromeda was one of many galaxies far beyond the boundaries of our own.

The Great Debate was brought to an end, but Hubble was still to make (or perhaps, more accurately, confirm) another seismic cosmological discovery. In 1929 he and Milton L. Humason formulated what is now known as Hubble's Law, by taking the Cepheid distances of several galaxies and combining them with the speed with which they had been observed to recede from us, as observed and measured by V. M. Slipher. The universe, they announced, was expanding. Though the

Georges Lemaître, originator of the Big Bang theory.

quantity of recession velocity is known as Hubble's constant, and the proportion of this velocity to intergalactic distance is known as Hubble's Law, the notion of expansion had been posited theoretically two years earlier, in 1927, by a Belgian Catholic priest and former graduate student in astronomy at the University of Cambridge named Georges Lemaître (1894–1966). Lemaître had drawn the idea from Einstein's theory of general relativity, providing the first observational estimate of what would be known as the Hubble constant. Published in the annals of the Scientific Society of Brussels, a journal hardly read outside Belgium, his theory was, at first, little known. It did come to Einstein's notice, but he was initially resistant to Lemaître's idea of an expanding universe. 'Your calculations are correct', he told the Belgian, 'but your physics is abominable.'

In 1931 a commentary on the article was published in the *Monthly Notices of the Royal Astronomical Society*, and with newfound attention Lemaître went further, proposing an idea that scientists have built on ever since: that our expanding universe could be traced back to a single point of origin, a finite moment in the past when all the mass of the universe was concentrated, where (and when) the fabric of time and space suddenly burst into existence. Lemaître called this the 'hypothesis of the primeval atom', or the Cosmic Egg – today we call this the Big Bang theory.

OPPOSITE: *'The Earth as it would appear in comparison with the flames shooting out from the Sun', from* G. E. Mitton's The Book of Stars for Young People *(1925).*

BREAKTHROUGHS OF THE TWENTIETH CENTURY, AND BEYOND

Though we now approach the modern era, and the end of this chronology, there should be no sense of deceleration. In fact, the twentieth century is often described as the century in which more progress was made in the science of astronomy, in line with technological advancements, than any other*. Following Einstein's theories and Hubble's discovery of galaxies beyond, the universe exploded in size (and with Hubble's Law supporting Lemaître's earlier theories 'explode' was indeed the right term). With Hubble's assertion that nebulae were other distant galaxies,

OPPOSITE: *In 1944, a female Japanese amateur astronomer named Hisako Koyama (1916–1997) began observing the Sun. In 1946 she became a staff observer at the Tokyo Science Museum and continued methodically drawing sunspots every day for forty years, providing one of the most valuable studies of solar activity ever made.*

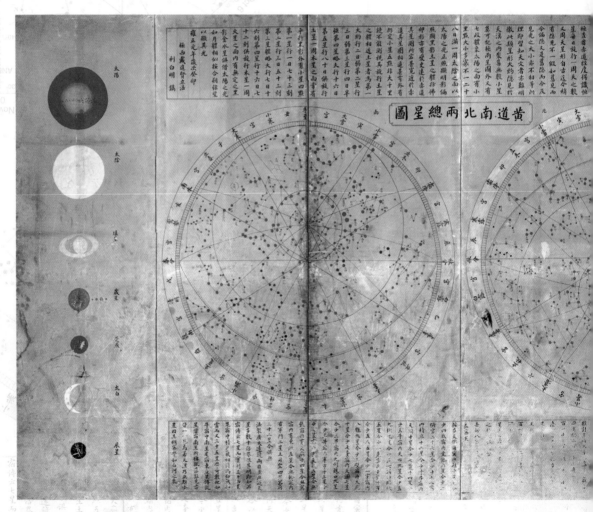

*This, of course, stirred up an unprecedented level of public fascination with space, even moving an American gentleman named A. Dean Lindsay to attempt to establish his legal ownership over the entirety of the universe beyond Earth. In 1937 Lindsay boldly filed his claim to 'the property known as planets, islands-of-space or other matter, henceforth to be known as 'A.D. Lindsay's archapellago [sic]' with the Superior Court of Ocilla, Georgia. 'Can you believe it?' he wrote in a letter to a friend shortly after filing the paperwork. 'That I own the Moon and the Sun, the stars, the comets, meteors, asteroids – everything, everywhere beyond this world?' (Unfortunately for Lindsay, and others with the same idea, the 1967 Outer Space Treaty, which established that sovereign claims cannot be made, would thwart such ambitions.)

BELOW: *A late nineteenth-century Japanese star map based on the observations of Ignaz Kögler (1680 –1746), a German Jesuit missionary.*

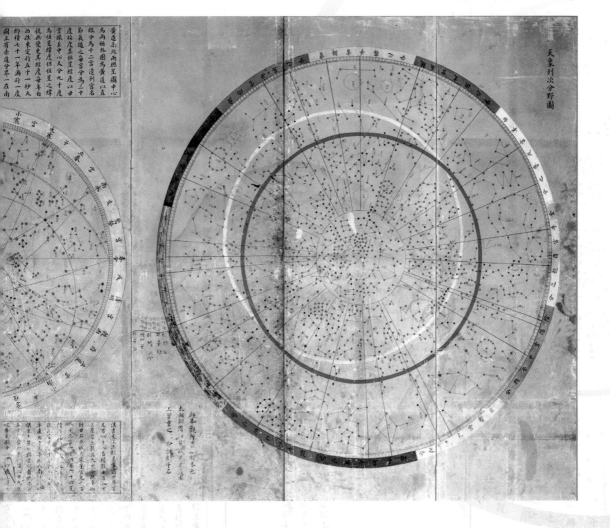

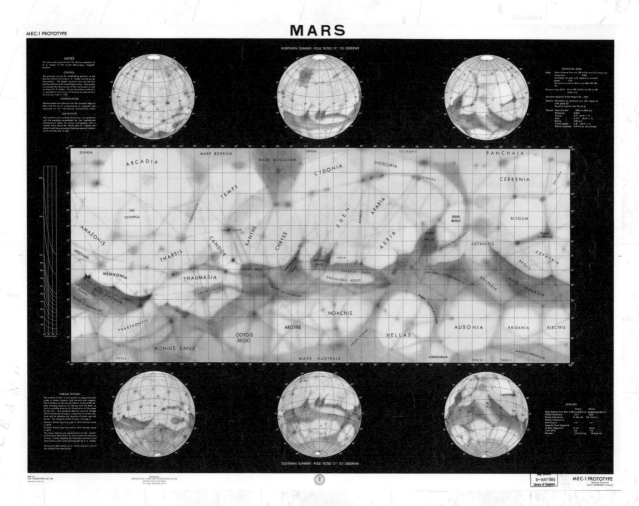

MARS

A 1962–1965 prototype map of the surface of Mars, in Mercatorial (flat) and spherical projections. This map in part draws on the observations of Percival Lowell (see Percival Lowell Spies Life on Mars entry on page 210).

the notion under which astronomers had laboured for thousands of years – that ours was the lone galaxy – was shattered. In fact, the estimated number of these galaxies continues to grow. In 1999 observations made with the Hubble Space Telescope (HST) produced the estimate of about 125 billion but, more recently, computer modelling suggests the number might be closer to 500 billion galaxies.

While both the ideas of an expanding universe and the introduction of a multitude of galaxies top the list of significant breakthroughs in twentieth-century astronomy, a close contender came in 1964, when the American radio astronomers Arno Penzias and Robert Woodrow Wilson discovered the cosmic microwave background (CMB), which provides strong evidence for the Big Bang as the origin of the universe. The CMB is a fascinating relic from the early stage in the creation of the universe known as the Recombination epoch, taking

place only 378,000 years after the Big Bang. This was the point when charged electrons and protons first became bound to form electrically neutral hydrogen atoms. The CMB takes the form of a faint electromagnetic radiation that fills all space and, as the earliest such radiation, provides us with data on an inchoate universe. With a suitably sensitive radio telescope, it is possible to detect this radiation as a weak glow in the dark spaces between stars. In the past, there has been an easier way to detect it in some form: until the switch was made to digital televisual broadcasts, about one per cent of the distorted static on televisions found between channels was made up of this background

A lunar reference mosaic, put together in November 1962 by the US Air Force.

~ 50 KM

radiation. Though the search for the CMB was begun in the 1940s, its discovery in 1964 by Penzias and Wilson was accidental, and earned them the Nobel Prize in Physics in 1978.

A greater, remaining mystery observable not in form but through its effect was first formally inferred in 1933 by the Swiss astrophysicist Fritz Zwicky, when he studied the Coma Cluster of galaxies. He realized that they were moving with a speed greater than could be accounted for by their mass, and estimated that the cluster had 400 times more mass than could be observed. There must, he thought, be a kind of *dunkle Materie* ('dark matter'), invisible to the eye, to explain this. Indeed it seems that most of the universe is made of a material that we cannot see. The visible, radiating celestial bodies account for only about 4 per cent of the mass in the universe. A hypothetical dark matter and 'dark energy' with a ubiquitous existence are implied by various observable gravitational effects that could occur only with the presence of more matter than is visible. Given the rotational velocity of spinning galaxies, without this huge amount of invisible mass present they would simply fly apart.

The idea was given its greatest reinforcement by the pioneering work of the American astronomer Vera Rubin (1928–2016), who uncovered the discrepancy between the predicted angular motion of galaxies, and the motion with which they were observed to possess. The peculiar motion of this 'galaxy rotation problem' phenomenon is today considered evidence of the existence of dark matter, confirmed through

When the Mariner 4 *spacecraft flew by Mars on 15 July 1965, it captured the first close-up images of another planet. The data was transmitted back to NASA, where it was to slowly be translated into a picture. Too impatient to wait, employees at the National Aeronautics and Space Administration's (NASA) Jet Propulsion Laboratory printed out the data in strips and frantically hand-coloured the assembled pieces, producing this image.*

the decades after Rubin's controversial results in the 1960s. Further support is provided by gravitational lensing, a bending of light predicted by Einstein's general theory of relativity, which was confirmed in 1979. In today's standard cosmological model, dark energy together with dark matter make up 95 per cent of total mass–energy content. While dark matter is yet to be observed, it's likely that it is an as-yet-undiscovered elementary particle, perhaps the hypothetical WIMP ('weakly interacting massive particles') or the MACHO ('massive astrophysical compact halo object'). (Astrophysicists enjoy a good acronym as much as anyone.)

While theoretical physicists obsessed over these challenges, our gaze penetrated ever farther into the secrets of the sky's dark ocean. In the late 1960s, the upcoming occurrence of a

To take this 2002 image of the deep cosmos, the HST peered through the centre of one of the most massive known galaxy clusters, called Abell 1689. The gravity of the cluster's trillion stars, and that of the mass of its dark matter, acted as a 3 million-light-year-wide lens in space, bending and magnifying the light of the distant galaxies behind it. A number of the faintest objects in the image are more than 13 billion light years away.

rare alignment of the outer planets, which happens only once every 175 years, spurred the creation of the *Voyager* probe programme to explore the outer solar system. Built by the Jet Propulsion Laboratory in southern California and funded and launched by NASA at Cape Canaveral, Florida, *Voyager 2* was the first to take flight on 20 August 1977, on a trajectory calculated to closely pass Jupiter, Saturn, Uranus and Neptune. *Voyager 1* followed shortly after, on 5 September 1977, on a tight and fast trajectory to allow a flyby of Saturn's moon Titan. This it achieved, but in doing so was shot out of the plane of the ecliptic, initiating a new journey. Meanwhile, in 1986 alone, five separate spacecraft were dispatched to Halley's Comet. Among these, the vessel *Giotto*, sent by the European Space Agency (ESA), reached a proximity of under 375 miles (604km) of the central mass of the comet and collected ten hours of data and images.

In 2012, *Voyager 1* became the first man-made object to enter interstellar space, having overtaken the slower deep-space probes *Pioneer 10* and *Pioneer 11* in the 1990s, and since 2013 has rocketed along with a velocity of 11 miles per second (17km/s) relative to the Sun. The spacecraft has captured close-up images of Jupiter's complex cloud forms and storm systems,

A map of the Apollo 11*'s landing location, signed by Buzz Aldrin.*

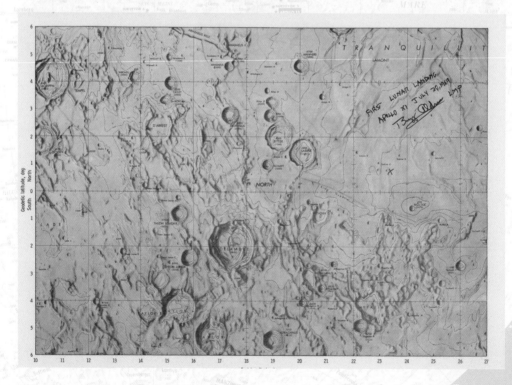

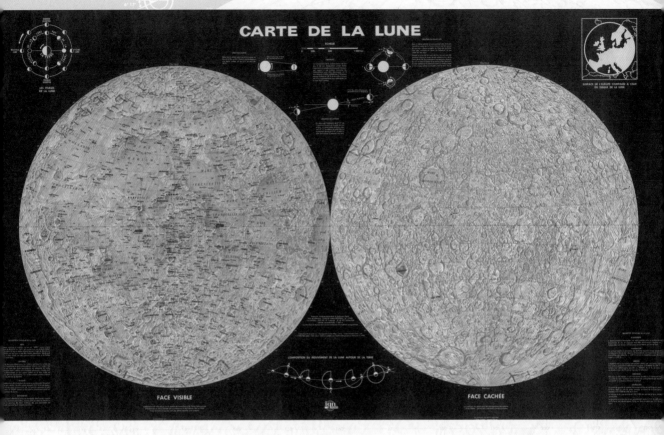

CARTE DE LA LUNE

FACE VISIBLE

FACE CACHÉE

revealed volcanic activity on its moon, Io, and discovered mysterious kinks and braids in Saturn's rings.* *Voyager 2* discovered a magnetic field around Uranus, and ten additional moons. As it flew past Neptune, it found another six moons, and vast auroras; and, in August 2018, NASA confirmed the existence of a 'hydrogen wall' at the outer edges of the solar system, first noticed by the two *Voyager* spacecraft in 1992.

Since 1990, when it was launched into a low Earth orbit, the HST has provided extremely high-resolution images** of the universe, beyond the distortion of the planet's atmosphere and with considerably lower background light than any telescope on the ground. Built by NASA, together with the ESA, it's the

A French map of the Moon created just after the first manned lunar landings by Apollo 11 *and* Apollo 12 *in 1969. It shows the landing sites of both craft, as well as those of previous unmanned missions of the Orbiter, Surveyor and Ranger Missions for NASA and the Russian Luna Missions.*

*Incidentally, rings aren't limited to planets. In 2014, for example, astronomers discovered rings around the asteroid Chariklo. It's unknown why such a small body would have them, but it's thought that perhaps they're collected fragments of a shattered moonlet.

** This resolution took a while to achieve. Soon after the launch, it was discovered that one of the Hubble's lenses failed to achieve sharp focus, thanks to a mirror with an aberration one-fiftieth the thickness of a human hair (the primary and secondary mirrors had been tested independently, but no one had tested the complete telescope before it was sent into orbit). The defective equipment was replaced by space-walking astronauts in 1993 at a cost of $900 million.

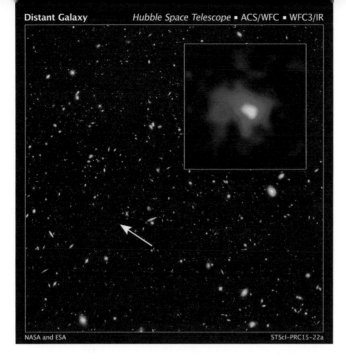

GN-z11, the farthest spectroscopically confirmed galaxy ever observed, identified as a very bright source in this image by the HST as part of CANDELS (Cosmic Assembly Near-infrared Deep Extragalactic Legacy Survey). The galaxy existed more than 13 billion years ago.

only telescope designed to be serviced in space by astronauts, and as such has had its life extended several times. Following its fifth servicing mission in 2009, the telescope is predicted to operate as late as 2040. With the instrumentation to observe in the near ultraviolet, visible and near-infrared spectra, the HST has allowed us the deepest view into space and time and facilitated numerous breakthroughs in astrophysics.

It's thanks to the HST, for example, that we made the accurate determination of the rate of expansion of the universe, through precise measurement of distances to Cepheid variable stars, refining the value of the Hubble constant. Before the launch of the HST, our estimates of the Hubble constant usually had a margin of error of up to 50 per cent – with the telescope, this was reduced to a margin of 10 per cent. The estimated age is now about 13.7 billion years, sharpened by the HST from previous predictions of 10 to 20 billion years. Using the HST to observe distant supernovae, it was also found that the expansion of the universe is likely accelerating. (Why exactly this is happening is unknown, but the most common explanation is dark energy.) It was with the HST that we realized that black holes are likely common to the centres of all galaxies and that the evidence for the presence of extrasolar planets around Sun-like stars was discovered. We have also managed to study objects far across the solar system, including the dwarf planets Pluto and Eris. More recently, on 3 March 2016, with Hubble data the discovery was made of the farthest known galaxy, GN-z11, at a distance of approximately 32 billion light years away.

Opposite: *The star cluster Pismis 24 lies in the heart of the large emission nebula NGC 6357, in the direction of the Scorpius constellation.*

The greatest images, though, are most likely to come. The planned scientific successor of the HST is the James Webb space telescope (JWST), named after the administrator of NASA 1961–1968. Yet to be launched at the time of writing, the telescope is due to take up its position in orbit some 930,000 miles (1,500,000km) from Earth in March 2021. Its eighteen hexagonal mirrors of gold-coated beryllium combine to make an enormous 21ft 4in- (6.5m-) diameter mirror (for comparison, the HST has a 'mere' 7ft 10in/2.4m mirror). With this the JWST will observe the farthest events and objects in the universe – the formation of the first galaxies, the births of distant stars and planets – as well as generate images of exoplanets and novae, and many other sights currently beyond the detective reach of current Earth- and space-based instruments. For all the astronomical innovations and revolutions of the past millennia, it is clear that there is no more thrilling a period of celestial discovery to witness than the one in which we currently exist.

ABOVE: *A 9 July 2013 mosaic of 102 Viking Orbiter images taken 1550 miles (2500km) from the surface of Mars, forming a perspective that one would have from a spacecraft. The main lateral feature visible here is the Valles Marineris ('Mariner Valley'), the largest canyon in the solar system at 2500 miles (4000km) long with a depth of up to 4 miles (6.5km).*

OPPOSITE: *The Pillars of Creation, one of the most famous images taken by NASA's HST, originally photographed in 1995. Part of an enormous star-forming region 6500 light years from Earth in the Eagle Nebula, the pillars are about five light years tall. Deep inside them, stars are being born.*

AFTERWORD

As to the metric for our expectations of the future, we need only look at the phenomenal rate of invention that has occurred in the relatively short amount of time since 1900 for a sense of what to anticipate. At the dawn of the twentieth century, astronomers made their calculations with logarithm tables and slide rules. To calculate a comet's orbit from a limited data set required three weeks of work – today this can be done in less than three minutes with computers. At that time, we thought ours to be the only planetary system; nothing was known of the inside of the atom, and the electron and neutron were undiscovered. Quantum mechanics was yet to unlock the study of spectroscopy and electromagnetic radiation. There was no understanding of special or general relativity, $E = mc^2$ had not been put to chalkboard, and no notions existed of nuclear fusion or fission. Today enormous radio telescopes litter the surface of Earth, and a fleet of gamma-ray, X-ray, ultraviolet and infrared space telescopes circle in orbit. Twelve men have walked on the surface of the Moon. Commercial space travel is on the verge of reality. Through both ground-based observatories and spectacularly spacecraft like the Kepler survey satellite, a total of 3726 exoplanets (planets beyond our solar system) have been confirmed throughout 2792 systems. Some of these exoplanets are so close to their stars that they're molten blobs lava; some are larger than Jupiter; and others are as small as Earth's moon. (Some orbit two stars and have become known as 'Tatooine' planets, named after

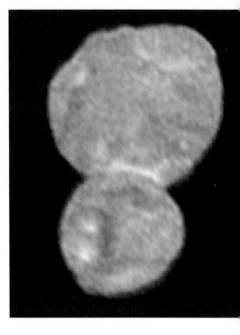

Ultima Thule at the far edge of the solar system, captured by the New Horizons *probe. The most distant object ever visited by a spacecraft.*

'Visions of the Future' image series produced by NASA/ JPL-Caltech, imagining the future of space travel.

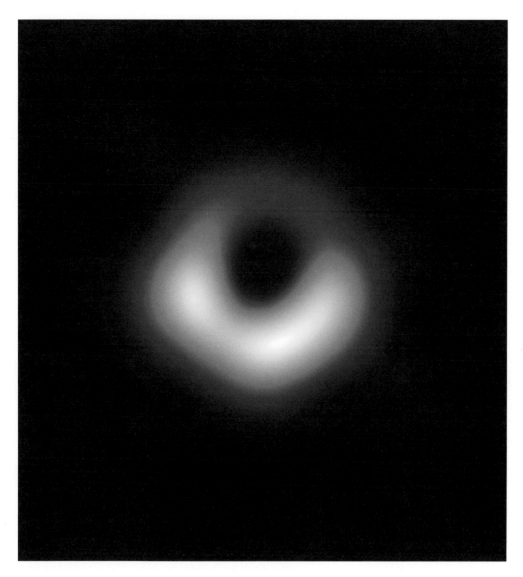

Luke Skywalker's home world.) It is now thought there are more planets than stars in the sky. Many more are expected to be found in the coming years with next-generation missions such as the National Aeronautics and Space Administration's (NASA) JWST.

At the time of writing, NASA's InSight robotic lander roams the surface of Mars to study its deep interior, having successfully landed on the planet on 26 November 2018; while another robotic NASA vehicle, the Parker Solar Probe spacecraft, is on its way to be the first to probe the outer corona of the Sun. Approaching within just 9.86 solar radii (4.3 million miles/ 6.9 million km) from the centre of the Sun, it is expected to hit –

'Seeing the unseeable' – on 10 April 2019 the US National Science Foundation made the historic announcement that the first image of the event horizon of a black hole (at the centre of the Messier 87 galaxy), something previously thought impossible to glimpse, had been successfully captured by the Event Horizon Telescope (EHT), an international array of ground-based radio telescopes.

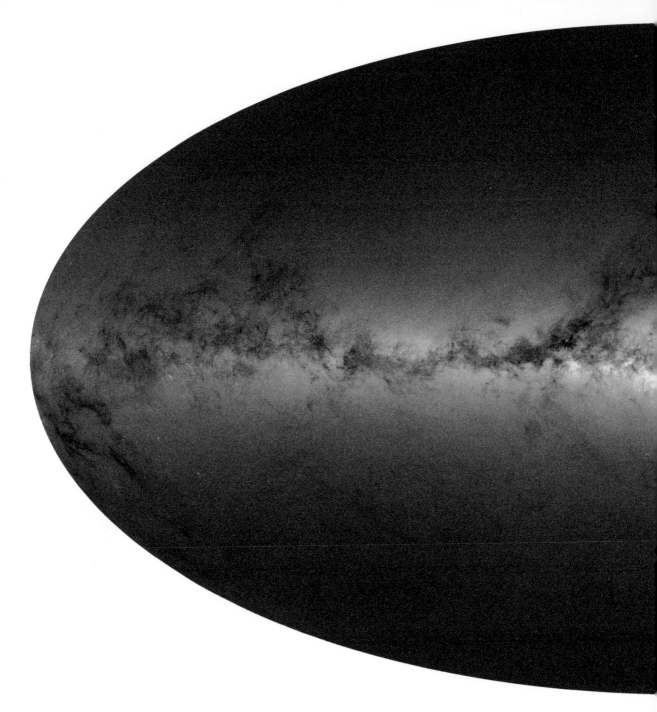

at closest approach – a speed of some 430,000mph (692,000km/h).
On 1 January 2019, the *New Horizons* probe, which flew past
Pluto in 2015, made the first flyby of a mysterious object of ice
and rock nicknamed Ultima Thule in the Kuiper Belt at the
extreme outer reaches of the solar system. By 2038, if it is still
functioning, the probe will share the mission of the *Voyager*
spacecraft and explore the outer heliosphere, perhaps crossing
the boundary into interstellar space.

The story of the sky continues to unfold. For us, arguably the most rewarded generation of our explorer species, it is impossible not to be swept up in the momentum of scientific progress and the excitement of boundless possibility. 'The known is finite, the unknown infinite,' wrote T. H. Huxley in 1887. 'Intellectually we stand on an islet in the midst of an illimitable ocean of inexplicability. Our business in every generation is to reclaim a little more land.'

The most detailed map of the Milky Way ever created. In 2018 the European Space Agency (ESA) published this image of our galaxy, and its neighbours, containing data on 1.7 billion stars, some as far as 8000 light years away. The information was gathered by the Gaia satellite over twenty-two months.

SELECT BIBLIOGRAPHY

Armstrong, K. (2005) *A Short History of Myth*, London: Canongate

Barentine, J. C. (2016) *The Lost Constellations*, London: Springer Praxis Books

Barrie, D. (2014) *Sextant...*, London: Collins

Benson, M. (2014) *Cosmigraphics*, New York: Abrams

Brunner, B. (2010) *Moon: A Brief History*, Yale: Yale University Press

Bunone, J. (1711) *Universal Geography*, London

Burl, A. (1983) *Prehistoric Astronomy and Ritual*, Aylesbury: Shire

Chapman, A. (2014) *Stargazers*, Oxford: Lion Books

Christianson, G. E. (1995) *Edwin Hubble: Mariner of the Nebulae*, New York: Farrar, Straus & Giroux

Clarke, V. (ed.) (2017) *Universe*, London: Phaidon

Crowe, M. J. (1994) *Modern Theories of the Universe from Herschel to Hubble*, New York: Dover

Crowe, M. J. (1990) *Theories of the World from Antiquity to the Copernican Revolution*, New York: Dover

Davie, M. & Shea, W. (2012) *Galileo: Selected Writings*, Oxford: Oxford University Press

Dekker, E. (2013) *Illustrating the Phaenomena: Celestial Cartography in Antiquity and the Middle Ages*, Oxford: Oxford University Press

Dunkin, E. (1869) *The Midnight Sky*, London: The Religious Tract Society

Feynman, R. (1965) *The Character of Physical Law*, Cambridge, MA: MIT Press

Ford, B. J. (1992) *Images of Science: A History of Scientific Illustration*, London: British Library

Galfard, C. (2015) *The Universe in Your Hand: A Journey Through Space, Time and Beyond*, London: Macmillan

Hawking, S. (1988) *A Brief History of Time*, London: Bantam

Hawking, S. (2016) *Black Holes: Reith Lectures*, London: Bantam

Hawking, S. (2006) *The Theory of Everything: The Origin and Fate of the Universe*, London: Phoenix

Hodson, F. R. (ed.) (1974) *The Place of Astronomy in the Ancient World*, Oxford: Oxford University Press

Hoskin, M. (2011) *Discoverers of the Universe: William and Caroline Herschel*, Princeton, NJ: Princeton University Press

Hoskin, M. (1997) *The Cambridge Illustrated History of Astronomy*, Cambridge: Cambridge University Press

Hubble, E. (1936) *The Realm of the Nebulae*, New Haven, CT: Yale University Press

Kanas, N. (2007) *Star Maps*, Chichester: Praxis

King, D. A. (1993) *Astronomy in the Service of Islam*, Aldershot: Variorum

King, H. C. (1955) *The History of the Telescope*, London: Charles Griffin

Kragh, H. S. (2007) *Conceptions of Cosmos*, Oxford: Oxford University Press

Lang, K. R. & Gingerich, O. (eds) (1979) *A Source Book in Astronomy and Astrophysics, 1900–1975*, Cambridge, MA: Harvard University Press

Mosley, A. (2007) *Bearing the Heavens: Tycho Brahe and the Astronomical Community of the Late Sixteenth Century*, Cambridge: Cambridge University Press

Motz, L. & Weaver, J. H. (1995) *The Story of Astronomy*, New York, NY: Plenum

Nakayama, S. (1969) *A History of Japanese Astronomy*, Cambridge, MA: Harvard University Press

Neugebauer, O. (1983) *Astronomy and History Selected Essays*, New York, NY: Springer-Verlag

Rooney, A. (2017) *Mapping the Universe*, London: Arcturus

Rovelli, C. (2016) *Seven Brief Lessons on Physics*, London: Penguin

Rovelli, C. (2011) *Anaximander*, Yardley: Westholme

Sagan, C. (1981) *Cosmos*, London: Macdonald

Snyder, G. S. (1984) *Maps of the Heavens*, New York, NY: Cross River Press

Sobel, D. (2017) *The Glass Universe*, London: Fourth Estate

Sobel, D. (2011) *A More Perfect Heaven: How Copernicus Revolutionized the Cosmos*, London: Bloomsbury

Sobel, D. (2005) *The Planets*, London: Fourth Estate

Stephenson, B. (1994) *The Music of the Heavens: Kepler's Harmonic Astronomy*, Princeton, NJ: Princeton University Press

Stott, C. (1991) *Celestial Charts*, London: Studio Editions

Thurston, H. (1993) *Early Astronomy*, New York, NY: Springer-Verlag

Van Helden, A. (1985) *Measuring the Universe: Cosmic Dimensions from Aristarchus to Halley*, Chicago, IL: University of Chicago Press

Whitfield, P. (2001) *Astrology*, London: British Library

Whitfield, P. (1995) *The Mapping of the Heavens*, London: British Library

Wulf, A. (2012) *Chasing Venus: The Race to Measure the Heavens*, London: Vintage

INDEX

ACKNOWLEDGEMENTS

I would like to express my deep appreciation to all who provided such indispensable help in the creation of this book: to Charlie Campbell at Kingsford Campbell, to Ian Marshall at Simon and Schuster, and Laura Nickoll and Keith Williams for their tireless work in creating such a beautiful book. Thank you to Franklin Brooke-Hitching for again enduring so many questions and to my entire family for their support, to Alex and Alexi Anstey, Daisy Laramy-Binks, Matt, Gemma and Charlie Troughton, Kate Awad, Katherine Parker, Georgie Hallett and Thea Lees, and to my friends at QI: John, Sarah and Coco Lloyd, Piers Fletcher, James Harkin, Alex Bell, Alice Campbell Davies, Jack Chambers, Anne Miller, Andrew Hunter Murray, Anna Ptaszynski, James Rawson, Dan Schreiber, Mike Turner and Sandi Toksvig.

I am especially grateful to those who have been so generous in providing and allowing the reproduction of the magnificent maps and other items collected here: to Barry Ruderman of Barry Lawrence Ruderman Antique Maps for his endless generosity in support of the project, to Massimo De Martini and Miles Baynton-Williams at Altea Antique Maps, to Daniel Crouch and Nick Trimming at Daniel Crouch Rare Books and Maps, Dreweatts Ltd and Carlton Rochell Asian Art, Steven Holmes and the Cartin Collection, the British Library, European Space Agency, National Aeronautics and Space Administration, the University of Ghent, the Metropolitan Museum of Art, the Library of Congress and the Wellcome Collection.

PICTURE AND MAP CREDITS

Alamy Pg 116–117; **Altea Antique Maps** Pg 42–43, 185 (bottom); **Anagoria** Pg 23, **Asahigraph** Pg 233 (top); **Ashmolean Museum, University of Oxford** Pg 79; **B. Still, NYU Archives** Pg 194 (top); **Barry Lawrence Ruderman Antique Maps** Pg 1, 6–7, 26, 56, 64–65 (both images), 66, 87, 98, 119, 121, 128, 134–135 (all images), 148–149 (all images), 150 (top), 162, 164, 166 (both images), 167 (top), 168–169, 173, 181 (bottom), 206 (bottom), 238, 239; **Bonhams** Pg 77; **British Library** Pg 22, 23, 36, 38, 40, 60–61, 67, 69, 89, 92, 100, 106, 123; **Cambridge University Library** Pg 158; **Cartin Collection** Pg 112 (bottom), 113 (top); **Colegota** Pg 25; **Jade Antique Maps, Asia** Pg 37 (bottom); **Dan Bruton, Ph.D., SFA Observatory, www.observatory.sfasu.edu** (repeated star map); **Daniel Crouch Rare Books and Maps** Pg 154–155, 215; **Dr Janos Korom** Pg 73; **Dreweatts Ltd and Carlton Rochell Asian Art** Pg 170–171; **Dublin: Chester Beatty Library (public domain)** Pg 37 (top); **Ed Dunens** Pg 15; **ESA/Gaia/DPAC** Pg 246–247; **European Space Agency/Hubble and NASA** Pg 177; **Fae** Pg 32; **bpk | Staatliche Kunstsammlungen Dresden | Elke Estel | Hans-Peter Klut** Pg 28–29; **Event Horizon Telescope collaboration et al. / National Science Foundation** Pg 245; **Getty Images** Pg 20; **Geographicus** Pg 146; **Glen McLaughlin Map Collection of California as an Island courtesy Stanford University Libraries** Pg 152–153; **Hans Bernhard** Pg 47; **Harvard University Library** Pg 218, 219; **Heidelberg University Library** Pg 13; **Heritage Image Partnership Ltd/Alamy Stock Photo** Pg 19; **Houghton Library, Harvard (public domain)** Pg 50, **Hunan Province Museum** Pg 39; **Institute of Astronomy Library, Cambridge** Pg 160, 161, 181 (top), 182 (bottom), 194 (bottom), 204 (top), 206 (top); **Joe Haythornthwaite** Pg 211 (bottom); **John Harding** Pg 33; **Leiden University** Pg 143; **Library of Congress** Pg 53, 55 (top and bottom), 57, 80, 102–103, 110–111, 114, 142, 144, 145, 151, 156, 178, 185 (top), 189, 198, 204 (bottom), 207 (bottom), 212–213, 220, 223, 234, 235; **Library of Congress, Geography and Map Division** Pg 63; **Library of Congress, Serial and Government Publications Division** Pg 226; **Livioandronico2013** Pg 118; **Marcus Bartlett** Pg 48; **Marsyas** Pg 51; **Metropolitan Museum of Art** Pg 3, 4–5, 10, 44, 46, 82–83 (all images), 104, 107, 108 (bottom), 125 (bottom), 193; **Minneapolis Museum of Art** Pg 141 (top); **Musee du Luxembourg (public domain)** Pg 140; **Museo nazionale della scienza e della tecnologia Leonardo da Vinci, Milano** Pg 108; **Myrabella** Pg 165 (top); **National Aeronautics and Space Administration (NASA), European Space Agency (ESA) and AURA/Caltech** Pg 24; **NASA/ESA** Pg 237; **NASA, ESA and Jesœs Maz Apellÿniz (Instituto de Astrofísica de Andalucía) – acknowledgement: Davide De Martin (ESA/Hubble)** Pg 240; **NASA, ESA, P. Oesch and I. Momcheva (Yale University), and the 3D-HST and HUDF09/XDF teams** Pg 241; **NASA, ESA and the Hubble Heritage Team (STScI/AURA)** Pg 242; **NASA/Johns Hopkins University Applied Physics Laboratory/Carnegie Institution of Washington** Pg 201; **NASA/JPL-Caltech** Pg 243, 244 (bottom three images); **National Aeronautics and Space Administration (NASA)/Johns Hopkins University Applied Physics Laboratory/Carnegie Institution of Washington** Pg 200; **NASA/Johns Hopkins University Applied Physics Laboratory/Southwest Research Institute** Pg 216, 244 (top); **NASA/JPL/Dan Goods** Pg 236, **National Gallery of Art** Pg 54; **National Diet Library of Japan** Pg 16, 232–233; **NLA** Pg 209 (top); **National Library of France (public domain)** Pg 18; **National Library of Medicine** Pg 81, 172, 186–187 (both images); **National Museum of Norway** Pg 70–71; **Österreichische Nationalbibliothek** Pg 124; **Paul K** Pg 112 (top 5 images); **Philip Pikart** Pg 25; **Pom²** Pg 76; **SenemmTSR** Pg 44; **Smithsonian** Pg 9, 125 (top), 138, 141 (bottom right), 141 (bottom left), 147, 150 (bottom), 174–175, 190, 191, 192, 221; **The al-Sabah Collection, Kuwait (public domain)** Pg 75; **The History of Chinese Science and Culture Foundation** Pg 41; **The Yorck Project** Pg 45; **totaltarian/imgur.com** Pg 8; **Tycho Brahe Museum, Ven** Pg 126 (bottom), 127; **University of Ghent** Pg 94–95 (all images); **University of Michigan** Pg 137; **virtusincertus** Pg 59; **Walters Art Museum (public domain)** Pg 93; **Wellcome Collection** Pg 11, 32, 48, 49, 129, 176, 182 (top); **Wellcome Library** Pg 84–85, 86; **Wikipedia.ru** Pg 91; **Xavier Caballe** Pg 208 (top left); **Zentralbibliothek Zürich** Pg 113 (bottom); **Zunkir** Pg 31

Page 1: *Planisfero Del Globo Celeste* by Giacomo Giovanni Rossi (1687)
Pages 4–5: Design for The Magic Flute – *The Hall of Stars in the Palace of the Queen of the Night*, 1847–1849 (after Karl Friedrich Schinkel)
Pages 6–7: Cellarius's *Planisphaerium Ptolemaicum* (1660)

First published in the United States in 2020 by Chronicle Books LLC.

Originally published in Great Britain in 2019 by Simon & Schuster UK Ltd.

Library of Congress Cataloging-in-Publication Data

Names: Brooke-Hitching, Edward, author.
Title: The sky atlas : the greatest maps, myths, and discoveries of the
    universe / Edward Brooke-Hitching.
Description: San Francisco : Chronicle Books, 2020. | "Originally published
    in Great Britain in 2019 by Simon & Schuster UK Ltd."
    —Colophon. | Includes bibliographical references and index.
Identifiers: LCCN 2019039280 | ISBN 9781797201184 (hardcover)
Subjects: LCSH: Stars—Atlases. | Astronomy—History. |
    Astronomy—History—Pictorial works. | Astronomy—Charts, diagrams, etc.
    | BISAC: HISTORY / Historical Geography
Classification: LCC G1000.2 .B76 2020 | DDC 520.9—dc23
LC record available at https://lccn.loc.gov/2019039280

Manufactured in Malaysia.

Editorial Director: Ian Marshall.
Design: Keith Williams, sprout.uk.com.
Project Editor: Laura Nickoll.
The author and publishers have made all reasonable efforts to contact copyright-holders for permission, and apologise for any omissions or errors in the form of credits given. Corrections may be made to future printings.

10 9 8 7 6 5 4 3

Chronicle Books LLC
680 Second Street
San Francisco, California 94107
www.chroniclebooks.com

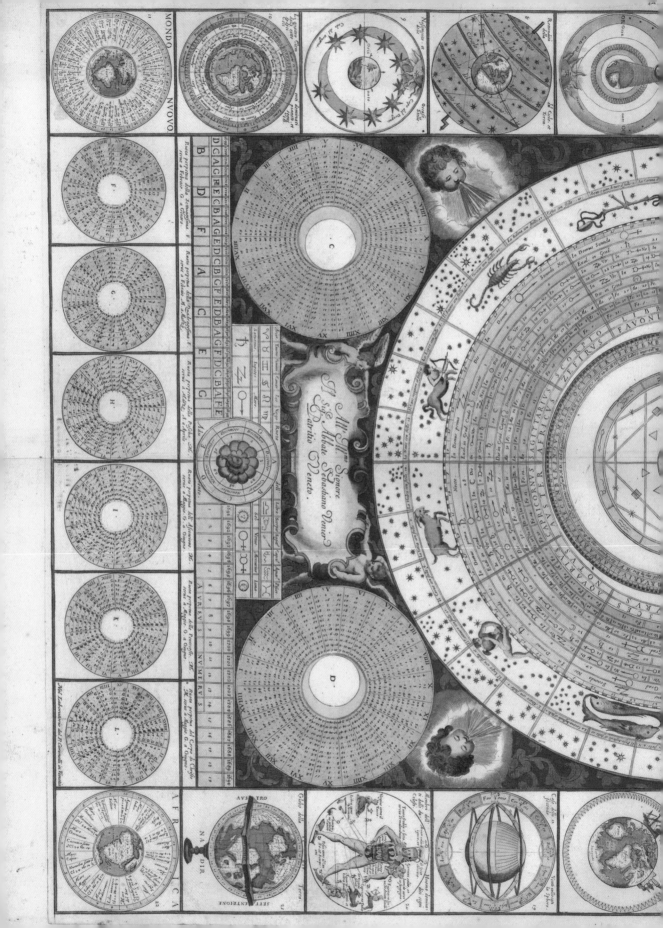